PENGUIN BOOKS

THE VILLA, THE LAKE, THE MEETING

'Lucid and compelling . . . a remarkable book' Saul Friedländer,
The Times Literary Supplement

'Roseman tells the story as if he were unfolding a thriller, and the
reader is left satisfied, perhaps understanding for the first time
what Wannsee was really about, as well as a little more about
how the great Nazi machine worked'
Julia Neuberger, *Irish Times*

'Fascinating . . . A lucid, penetrating and well-researched
study . . . This is probably the most persuasive summary so far'
Frank McLynn, *Independent*

'Partly a mystery story . . . a lively contribution to work on a
terrifying period in history. It is no simplistic account – chaos
and uncertainty are the very "stuff" of history – but, throughout
the book, we are forced to recognize the very ordinariness of
these men as we follow, step by step, the diverse routes they
followed in their will to destroy' Joanna Bourke, *New Statesman*

'A gripping scholarly investigation' *Observer*

'There is, to my knowledge, no book that brings together more
masterfully in less than 200 pages the daunting problems and
massive research on the Holocaust that Mark Roseman's account
of the notorious Wannsee Conference. Concise, accessible, yet
comprehensive, this is a most illuminating study of the
cold-blooded planning and execution of the most horrific crime
of the twentieth century' V. R. Berghahn

'A painstaking and timely reminder of the Nazis' uniquely
revolting combination of murder, lies and bumbling
ordinariness' Eric Jacobs, *The Times*

ABOUT THE AUTHOR

Mark Roseman is Professor of Modern History at the University of Southampton. Educated at Cambridge and Warwick, he has published widely on many aspects of German history. His books include *Recasting the Ruhr* (1992), *Generations in Conflict* (1995) and *The Past in Hiding* (2000), which won the Fraenkel Prize in Contemporary History for 2000 and the *Jewish Quarterly*–Wingate Literary Prize for Non-Fiction for 2001.

MARK ROSEMAN

The Villa, the Lake, the Meeting

WANNSEE AND THE FINAL SOLUTION

PENGUIN BOOKS

PENGUIN BOOKS

Published by the Penguin Group
Penguin Books Ltd, 80 Strand, London, WC2R ORL, England
Penguin Putnam Inc., 375 Hudson Street, New York, New York 10014, USA
Penguin Books Australia Ltd, 250 Camberwell Road, Camberwell, Victoria 3124, Australia
Penguin Books Canada Ltd, 10 Alcorn Avenue, Toronto, Ontario, Canada M4V 3B2
Penguin Books India (P) Ltd, 11, Community Centre, Panchsheel Park, New Delhi – 110 017, India
Penguin Books (NZ) Ltd, Cnr Rosedale and Airborne Roads, Albany, Auckland, New Zealand
Penguin Books (South Africa) (Pty) Ltd, 24 Sturdee Avenue, Rosebank 2196, South Africa

Penguin Books Ltd, Registered Offices: 80 Strand, London, WC2R ORL, England

www.penguin.com

First published by Allen Lane The Penguin Press 2002
Published in Penguin Books 2003
3

Copyright © Mark Roseman, 2002
All rights reserved

The moral right of the author has been asserted

Printed in England by Clays Ltd, St Ives plc

Contents

Acknowledgements

Thanks to all who provided helpful comments, suggestions or discussions, above all Hans-Christian Jasch, Norbert Kampe and Peter Klein, as well as Volker Berghahn, David Cesarani, Richard Evans, Christian Gerlach, Peter Longerich, K-D. Schmidt, Nicholas Stargardt, Peter Witte and my ever-helpful editor, Simon Winder. The staff at the Wiener Library, London and the Haus der Wannsee-Konferenz, Berlin (details of which can be found in English at www.ghwk.de) were particularly helpful in providing materials. Thanks, too, to Peter Robinson of Curtis Brown for his role in shaping the project. Some of the time writing this book was spent as a guest of Michigan State University, and I am very grateful for the hospitality I received. I am grateful also to the University of Southampton for allowing me the time to write the book.

My biggest debt is to Ann Larabee – for our many helpful discussions, for valuable stylistic and structural advice particularly in the closing stages of writing, and for providing, along with Jacob, Abigail and Kate, the emotional centre that made writing possible. This book is dedicated to her.

I

'Perhaps the most shameful document'

It was in March 1947, collecting information for the Nuremberg trials, that staff of the US prosecutor made the discovery.[1] Stamped *'Geheime Reichssache'* – 'Secret Reich matter' – and tucked away in a German Foreign Office folder, were the minutes of a meeting. The meeting had involved fifteen top Nazi civil servants, SS and Party officials and had taken place on 20 January 1942, in a grand Berlin villa on the shores of Lake Wannsee. The US officials had stumbled across the only surviving copy of the minutes, no. 16 out of an original thirty.

The minutes, or 'Wannsee Protocol' (in deference to the German term for minutes – *Protokoll*), as they soon came to be known, consist largely of a presentation by the head of the Nazi security service and chief of the German security police, Reinhard Heydrich. Heydrich surveys the measures undertaken towards Jews up to 1941, counts up all the Jews remaining in Axis, occupied, neutral and enemy Europe, and outlines a plan to 'evacuate' those Jews to the east. There is an extended discussion of how to deal with the half-Jew, the quarter-Jew, the Jew married to the gentile, the war-decorated Jew. While Heydrich's proposal is to comb Europe from west to east, the representative for the German administration of Poland makes a plea for the programme to begin in his patch. They had so many useless Jews in Poland. Despite the euphemism of evacuation, the minutes unmistakably contain a plan for genocide – formulated in sober, bureaucratic language, deliberated on in civilized surroundings in a once cosmopolitan suburb of Berlin. Serious, intelligent men had conferred together and delved into the details of the half-Jew, the quarter-Jew.

In 1947 the man in charge of prosecuting the German ministries was Robert Kempner, a former German(-Jewish) civil servant who had emigrated to the US in the 1930s. When the Protocol was unearthed, Kempner rushed to his boss, General Telford Taylor, to show what he had found. 'Is such a thing possible?' Taylor asked.[2] Both men knew they had discovered 'perhaps the most shameful document of modern history'.[3] There has never been a bleaker rendition of the orderly governance of murder. To this day the Wannsee Protocol remains the most emblematic and programmatic statement of the Nazi way of doing genocide.

Yet the Protocol is a deeply mysterious document. On the face of it, it captures the moment when the Nazis decided to eliminate the Jews. The prosecutors believed they had found the Rosetta stone of Nazi murder[4] and the Wannsee Protocol still figures as this in popular imagination today.[5] But historians have long argued that it cannot be what it seems. For one thing, Hitler was not there, and those present were too junior to decide on genocide. Above all, the timing seems wrong. The mass murder of Soviet Jews had begun half a year earlier. Jews had been gassed at Chelmno since early December 1941. The Belżec extermination camp was already under construction. So what then was the purpose of the gathering at Wannsee? Historians have rather struggled to deal with it.

Most have discounted the idea that a new plan had been tabled and have interpreted the meeting as an exercise in self-aggrandizement on the part of its convenor, Reinhard Heydrich. If this were correct, the Protocol's historical significance would be simply that it offers a clear picture of matters long decided elsewhere. Yet such an interpretation, while understandable in view of the shootings and gassings under way, does little to explain the Protocol's claim that the meeting was necessary to establish a 'comprehensive solution of the Jewish question' and above all that at the time of the meeting that solution had not yet begun. Perhaps the biggest point of consensus among historians until recently, therefore, was, as Eberhard Jäckel has argued, that 'the most remarkable thing about the Wannsee conference is that we do not know why it took place'.[6]

But the Protocol's macabre mystery goes deeper still. Even if we knew why the meeting was called, would that render it any more intelligible? Would we then be able to account for its mixture of procedure and prejudice, sober planning and ideologically motivated murder? Can we ever make sense of the devilish parody of administrative precision, delineating between the quarter-Jew (to be vetted), the half-Jew (to be sterilized if 'lucky'), or the full Jew (to be 'evacuated')? In other words, how was it possible, on a snowy January day in Berlin, to deliberate so calmly and carefully about genocide?

The Wannsee Protocol is emblematic of the Holocaust in another sense too. On the one hand, the Protocol exists, its authenticity undeniable, its leaden matter-of-factness as unanswerable as it is unfathomable.[7] It reminds us that the Holocaust is the best-documented mass murder in history. Bureaucracy was its hallmark, after all. Despite Nazi efforts to destroy the evidence, huge quantities of records were collected after the war, first by the legal teams of the various post-war trials, later by historians. During the war the Allies eavesdropped on German communications, and now their transcripts too are accessible. After 1945 thousands of testimonies were given in courtroom hearings and conversations with historians that together have opened up, as documents never could, the inner workings of the different planets orbiting in the Nazi universe of murder – forced labour, extermination camps and death marches.

Yet when it comes to understanding why and how the process was undertaken, the documentation is much less complete. Key papers have been destroyed. Many of the files belonging to the Reich Security Main Office, the body headed by Reinhard Heydrich – the man who called the Wannsee conference – have not been found and probably no longer exist. At the very top of the Nazi system there were no files anyway. Hitler never put commands on Jewish matters in writing; Himmler, too, was extraordinarily cautious. Moreover, the decision to carry out such an action in the middle of a major war is so macabre, so counter-intuitive, that a paper trail that would otherwise suffice to certificate the parentage of an idea or a policy is here not enough. That is why the present book opens not with a reconstruction of the conference itself but with the discovery of the Protocol, as a reminder that what we have is a document. There is no camera-eye view. Why did Heydrich select this particular group of participants? What was his original agenda? Why did his invitees attend and what did they say that is not in the minutes? On all of these things, we have to speculate.

The gaps in the record, but even more the questions Wannsee raises, force us to cast our net far wider than the meeting itself. After all, the issue is only partly: what was it that these men got up to on 20 January 1942? It is even more: how on earth did they get to that point? In particular, the Protocol's claim that the groundwork for the Final Solution had still not been prepared in January 1942 raises with peculiar force a question accompanying the entire history of the Holocaust: was the descent into genocide the result of some long-established plan? This question is difficult to answer partly because of the ambiguous character of Hitler's command. In general terms and particularly in relation to the Final Solution it is often unclear how binding and precise his orders were. What is more, the Nazi war on Jews in the nine years between Hitler's seizure of power and the Wannsee conference was characterized by a paradoxical combination of constant energy and changing purpose that is very hard to interpret.

During the 1970s and early 1980s historians were particularly sensitive to these questions of coherence and intention. Some readers will know of the debates between the 'intentionalists' and the 'structuralists'.[8] The former emphasized the clarity of Hitler's plans and his control over both people and events. The latter saw Hitler as less decided and less interventionist, and believed it was his subordinates' struggle for power in a chaotic political system that tipped the regime over the edge. The research generated in the context of these debates was enormously valuable, but in the process Wannsee became more, not less, of a puzzle.

This was not because of the polarization of interpretations per se. Most historians felt free to take the middle ground.[9] The best work came from 'moderate functionalists' who acknowledged Hitler was not always sure what he wanted and was often not in the hot seat, but concluded that in the end it was his finger on the button.[10] In such accounts Hitler crosses the Rubicon in July, August or September 1941. The Wannsee conference's meaning and timing thus remained elusive. The conceptual framework of the intentionalist-functionalist debate bedevilled even the half-way positions. In so far as there was a clear intention, it was Hitler's; in so far as there was wider participation, it was attributed to secondary motives: some authors – none more influential than Raul Hilberg[11] – emphasized the blind obedience of a bureaucracy; others, following Hans Mommsen and Martin Broszat, foregrounded the pulls and pushes of a deformed political system.[12] One does not have to subscribe to the view of a unique German 'eliminatory anti-Semitism' to agree with Daniel Goldhagen that such models of 'unmotivated' participation are wanting as an explanation for the trajectory and outlook of the men round the Wannsee table.[13]

Over the last decade and a half new research on the Holocaust has made Wannsee easier to place within the wider project of genocide. Writers such as Saul Friedländer, Ian Kershaw and others have provided subtle and penetrating accounts of the balance between leadership and followers, control and improvisation, that make the mixture of planfulness and planlessness easier to grasp.[14] Recent work by Ulrich Herbert and Peter Longerich, among others, has helped to rediscover the shared values and ideology of Hitler and followers, values not initially genocidal, but without which Wannsee could never have happened.[15] Finally, and perhaps most pertinent, the last few years have seen regional studies of the Holocaust in Poland and the former Soviet Union, many of them from younger German historians such as Christoph Dieckmann, Christian Gerlach, Dieter Pohl and Thomas Sandkühler, that draw on the vast amount of material hitherto locked up in Soviet Bloc archives, and help to fill the gaps in the papers at the centre.[16] As a result of this work we can see that in a curious feedback process, in some respects not unfamiliar from government policy on other matters and in other places – but horrifically out of place here – the deed of murder begat the idea of genocide as much as the other way around. Wannsee emerges as an important act of closure in the process of turning mass murder into genocide. Telling that story is the prime aim of this book.

The book therefore opens with two chapters that set the scene for Wannsee. The first sketches in very briefly the mixture of strong leadership and hesitancy, energy and chaos, purposefulness and apparent lack of direction that characterized the drift towards genocide in the years up to 1941. The second examines more closely the evidence for a clear decision on the Final Solution in the months leading up to the Wannsee conference. The remaining two chapters look at the conference itself and its aftermath. In all this, there is, of course, one huge omission. There is nothing here about the victims of this process. Instead, this is a book trying to paint a picture of how, on 20 January 1942, fifteen educated men met to talk about genocide.

2

Mein Kampf to mass murder, 1919–41

Mein Kampf *and murder*

The close parallels between Hitler's repeated threats in the 1920s and Jews' eventual fate in the 1940s might well suggest that the Wannsee Protocol was, in effect, merely a typewritten digest of *Mein Kampf*. But the journey to Wannsee is more complicated and ambiguous than that. Hitler's writings in the 1920s certainly show him obsessed by the 'Jewish problem', far more so than by Bolshevism or Marxism. Other groups too fell foul of Hitler's racial vision – syphilitics, alcoholics and criminals should be isolated and sterilized, perhaps even 'amputated' from German society[1] – but only the Jews were seen as conspiring against the nation. The Jews were a racial rather than religious enemy and conversion to Christianity thus pointless. They were a rootless, international force, seeking to undermine Germany from within and without through the twin agencies of international Bolshevism and international finance capital. From the early 1920s until his death, Hitler remained wedded to the idea that 'Juda' was 'the plague of the world'[2] and that Germany's future health depended on eradicating this plague.

Hitler's language is extraordinarily violent and bloodthirsty, redolent with metaphors of plague and parasite. The Jew was variously a 'maggot', a plague, a blood-sucking spider, a rat, a harmful bacillus or a vampire.[3] In *Mein Kampf* and in his speeches he talks of 'extermination' (*Vernichtung*) and even of gassing Jews; the outcome of the

First World War might well have been different, he said, if, instead of the men at the front, 10,000–15,000 leading Hebrews had been exposed to poison gas. The rhetoric is deeply disturbing and deeply ominous. But did Hitler actually have a clear conception of genocide and the intent to unleash it? The problem is that he was both realist and fantasist. The realist Hitler will not have thought of genocide as a feasible proposition. In 1925 he even alluded to the tactical character of his anti-Semitism. It was politically expedient to 'select but one enemy that everyone can recognize: he is the only guilty one . . . And this enemy is the Jews.'[4] The gangster and self-publicist Hitler will have relished the threatening sound of murder. Will the obsessive anti-Semite Hitler have entertained the fantasy of genocide? Looking back in 1941 and again at the end of the war, Hitler claimed that he had followed a straight path.[5] Yet on other occasions he acknowledged that *Mein Kampf* was no blueprint.[6]

How literally then should we take the vocabulary of extermination? After all, the concept of *Vernichtung* (a word which can mean destruction or eradication as well as extermination) was part of the wider political vocabulary in contexts in which the physical extinction of a group or a people was inconceivable.[7] The extensive parasitological metaphors have also to be seen in the context of an established radical discourse on the dangers of the Jewish presence. Paul de Lagarde, writing before the turn of the century, was already talking about the elimination of bacilli.[8] Some authors[9] have argued that there is therefore a continuity of intent stretching from writers such as Wilhelm Marr, Eugen Dühring and de Lagarde through to the Holocaust, but it seems extremely unlikely that Hitler's precursors really conceived of the mass biological destruction of hundreds of thousands or millions of individuals.

True, unlike a Marr or a Dühring, Hitler wrote with the First World War behind him, an experience that rendered conceivable the idea of millions dying as a result of the modern technology of death. It was after the war, Hitler said, that he learned to hate.[10] But his talk about gassing at the front was more blackmail than genocide. A few thousand hostages should be gassed to keep the rest quiescent. This is lethal enough, and rested on some crucial assumptions in Hitler's mental universe. Above all, Jews – the international force – had been in league with the enemy. That was why holding them as hostages in wartime might be particularly effective. But it does not suggest that the gas chambers of the 1940s were being imagined in the 1920s. In other words, there is no straight line to be drawn from Hitler's language of extermination to the genocidal plans of Wannsee. What we can say is that his rhetoric was murderously ambiguous. At the core was a commitment to getting the Jews out of Germany. 'The final aim,' Hitler wrote as early as 1919, 'must be the uncompromising removal of the Jews altogether.'[11] Surrounding the core was an ultimately catastrophic combination of gangsterish threats and murderous flights of fantasy.

Emigration and ambiguity

The same murderous ambiguity is evident when we switch our search for Wannsee's antecedents from the ideology of the 1920s to the policy of the 1930s. The ferocious anti-Semitism is obvious. From the moment Hitler acceded to power on 30 January 1933, Germany's Jews found themselves in the firing line. Continuing a pattern all too familiar from the weeks and months before Hitler was appointed chancellor, Nazi paramilitary (SA) and Hitler Youth members embarked on kicking and window-smashing sprees against Jewish targets. Within a few weeks, the regional Party chief (gauleiter) had taken up the campaign, stoking up organized attacks against Jewish businesses in one district after another.[12] A national, government-sponsored boycott of Jewish businesses at the beginning of April was followed by a purge of the civil service. Between 1933 and 1934 Jews were removed almost completely from German public life. After a brief lull, and with a further interruption during the months around the Berlin Olympic Games, the period 1935–7 saw a whole raft of further measures: Jews lost their citizenship,[13] were forbidden to have sexual relations with Aryans and were denied access to almost every public amenity. Towards the end of 1937 the intensity of the assault was ratcheted up several more notches. Jews were denied virtually any possibility of earning an independent living. The regime massively increased the pressure to emigrate. On 'Kristallnacht', 9 November 1938, Nazi brutality smashed through the doors and windows of almost every remaining Jewish home and business in the country. By the outbreak of the Second World War Germany had travelled an astonishingly long way down the road of persecution; the country's remaining Jews were a huddled, terrified remnant, living off savings and communal charity.

Yet the tide of discriminatory measures that engulfed the Jewish community with such breathtaking speed was sweeping towards the goal of a Jew-free society, not murder. After the Anschluβ with Austria in 1938, special centres were established in Vienna and later in Berlin to 'facilitate' Jewish emigration. The aim was not even vaguely to try to hold Jews in readiness for later disposal; on the contrary – the further from Germany's reach the better. Late in April 1940 the hardliners in the Reich Security Main Office laid down that Jewish emigration should be pursued during the war with increased emphasis.[14] The energy expended makes no sense if policy even secretly was aiming at murder. The Nazis' principal goals up to the war were to remove Jewish influence, remove Jewish wealth and remove the Jews from Germany. It was thus to be a very twisted road to Wannsee.[15]

More worrying than either the overt or covert goals behind anti-Jewish measures, however, was the capacity for brutality and violence evinced in actions large and small. The callousness of the legal assault on the Jews was breathtaking. On a much broader front the regime suspended most of the legal rights and safeguards contained in the Weimar constitution. Striking, too, was the readiness to deploy violence, a readiness that reached its gruesome highpoint on Kristallnacht. True, Kristallnacht did not represent the 'norm' of Nazi Jewish policy in the 1930s. It led in some respects to a rejection of overt violence on German streets, particularly by the institutions that were to become dominant in shaping Jewish policy thereafter. But a regime that could sanction Kristallnacht, it might well be argued, was capable of sanctioning anything.

Hitler and his henchmen

At Wannsee fifteen men from a variety of different institutions and agencies met to talk about murder. The relationships between them, and their involvement in anti-Jewish action, were decisively formed in the 1930s. More than any specific goals laid down in that decade, it was the emerging 'syndrome' of eager subordination, shared racist values and competitive cooperation in pursuit of those values that provided the most disastrous omen for the future.

Some historians, as we know, have seen in the competition between Hitler's satraps the driving force that eventually led to genocide. Anti-Semitic measures, so the argument runs, swept forward with neither a coherent vision nor a master hand to guide them. Hitler, a late riser, slow diner, rambling speaker and political dilettante, did not give Jewish measures particularly close attention. Never a man to create clarity where confusion might keep his subordinates on the hop, he also did not nominate any one person to take charge of Jewish affairs. In Nazi Germany in general, the lack of clear responsibilities and the overlap between inherited state institutions, new Party agencies and the hybrid bodies in between, encouraged competition for power. Jewish policy provided the perfect arena for ambitious men to assert their ideological credentials. It was known to enjoy Hitler's particular regard and there was never going to be serious opposition: there was no Jewish 'bloc' enfranchised within the power-system to counter initiatives. Since the regime also lacked democratic institutions to absorb grievances and demands for change, the Jewish arena was the perfect playpen in which grassroots radicals, frustrated at their lack of influence in the new system, could be allowed to kick and shout.

In this context Hitler has sometimes even been seen as a restraining force. 'Whenever he was confronted with a choice between two courses of action,' writes the historian Hans Mommsen, 'he would favour the less extreme solution rather than play the part of revolutionary agitator.'[16] In shaping the Nuremberg Laws, for example, Hitler did not always take the radical line. On the face of it, the Laws offer little evidence of coherent planning either. Cobbled together at the last minute, they were delivered as an impromptu place filler conjured up when a major foreign policy statement at the end of the Nuremberg rally had to be dropped.[17] The explosion of violence on Kristallnacht, to take another example, has been seen as another impromptu measure, and one not ordered by Hitler. Historians have drawn attention to Josef Goebbels's role in unleashing the catastrophe, concerned as he was to regain profile following the disgrace surrounding his recent affair with an actress.[18]

The broad participation of different groups in making policy is indeed highly significant, as were the opportunities opened by the fluid Nazi system to ambitious young men. The Wannsee conference itself was called by a power-hungry Heydrich, seeking to bring his counterparts into line. Yet, the image of the satraps jostling for power is in two senses in need of revision. For one thing, Hitler's influence was greater than this suggests. It is not in dispute that his authority rapidly became unrivalled. He was the head of the Nazi Party and the chancellor, after 1934 also inheritor of the presidential powers. More than that, his massive popular acclaim and the unrivalled loyalty and devotion he enjoyed from the Party's hard core became the central elements in the new system's unwritten constitution. Together they put him beyond criticism or competition. Hitler, true enough, was often slow to act. But the system became so attuned to his signals that a raised finger was enough. He was at pains not to tie his name too closely to anti-Semitic measures, but it was he even so who frequently set the agenda and moved it on. The Nuremberg Laws, for example, might have been rushed through at the end, but they were the culmination of two years in which Hitler had regularly flagged up the citizenship question and the Interior Ministry had given it much thought.[19] He did not really play the moderate either since it was he who sabotaged Interior Ministry attempts to exclude half- and quarter-Jews from the Laws.[20]

Above all, it was Hitler who set the radical new tone in the second half of the 1930s. While pushing through economic mobilization for war, taking greater risks in foreign policy and increasingly pushing aside or demoting the conservative elites with whom he had been in partnership, Hitler also repeatedly emphasized to narrower and wider Party and official circles the importance of removing the Jews. 'The Jews must get out of Germany,' noted Goebbels after one such harangue from Hitler, 'yes, out of the whole of Europe. That will still take some time. But it will and must happen. The Führer is firmly decided upon it.'[21]

Even when initiatives came from elsewhere, Hitler often exerted 'downward causation'. He stifled moves he did not want or whose time he felt to be inopportune, while encouraging others. In February 1936, for example, the Nazi leader in Switzerland, Wilhelm Gustloff, was assassinated by a Jewish student. The Olympic Winter Games were pending and Hitler, recognizing the diplomatic capital to be made from restraint, forbade public protests. What a dramatic demonstration of his power, that there were none.[22] Two and a half years later, when the legation secretary Ernst vom Rath was killed in Paris by the Polish Jew Herschel Grynszpan, the 'spontaneous reaction' was Kristallnacht. Here again, recent research has shown that, contrary to historians' emphasis on Goebbels as pace-maker, Hitler himself probably gave the signal for action.[23] Hermann Göring certainly thought so. Responding to the suggestion that the perpetrators should be brought to book, Göring asked, ' "You want to punish Hitler?" '[24]

Yet Hitler's fantasies would never have taken shape without the energetic participation of others, participation that helped to refine and reshape his own goals. Hitler's guidance, though decisive, was intermittent; during the war it became much more so. Raul Hilberg's list of the principal players in the Jewish Question includes twenty-seven different agencies, the most important of which would be represented at Wannsee.[25] In very general terms, three main groups were involved: the Party, the ministries (most of whose personnel at least initially were inherited from the previous regime) and Himmler's SS-police empire.

In the early years Jewish policy was shaped largely by interaction between Party pressure, Hitler's signals and ministerial actions. But after 1936 two new players emerged. One was Göring, whose hybrid economic empire, the Four-Year Plan organization, played a major role in mobilizing the economy for war until 1942–3. In the second half of the 1930s Göring attained de facto leadership on the Jewish question. It was he who chaired the infamous post-Kristallnacht meeting at which Heydrich was charged with developing a comprehensive emigration policy to clear Germany of Jews. But it was Himmler's SS-police empire and, under him, Heydrich's security police and security service fiefdoms, that were to be crucial in developing the Final Solution.

Himmler had originally been appointed Reich leader of the SS in January 1929, when the 280-man organization was little more than Hitler's bodyguard. By 1931, with a membership running into some thousands, the SS were given the dual function of police force and elite troop. Himmler sought to craft the body into a racial elite, requiring from its officers proof of 'pure Aryan' descent back to 1750, and taking a personal interest in vetting their brides. After 1933, in a characteristic Nazi administrative muddle, Himmler added to his SS responsibilities by piecemeal acquisitions of first the Bavarian and later other regional police authorities. Only in 1936 was his position formalized. Nominally Himmler was subordinate to the Ministry of the Interior, but in reality his leadership of the SS and close links to Hitler denied the ministry any chance of control. The Reich Security Main Office (Reichssicherheitshauptamt, RSHA) was created in 1939, formally joining the SS security service (Sicherheitsdienst, SD) and the security police (criminal police and secret state police, Gestapo).

As Himmler swept from head of Hitler's bodyguard to master of the Reich security forces, his subordinate Reinhard Heydrich, the architect of Wannsee, rose in his wake. Appointed in 1932 to head the SD, Heydrich brought the security police, including the Gestapo, under his wing, and in 1939 became the RSHA's first chief. Until 1935 the security services devoted most of their attention to the left and the churches. But responding to Hitler's signals, in the course of 1936 Heydrich expanded the SD's Jewish section. After he acquired control of the Gestapo, he established an analogous department there for Jews, freemasons and emigrants. In Heydrich's conception, the SD was to be the Reich's think-tank on Jewish matters, the Gestapo its front-line combatant. When Hitler's stance on Jews sharpened, so did the SD's interest in the question. After the Anschluβ with Austria in 1938, Heydrich created a central office for Jewish emigration in Vienna to streamline removal of Jews. But it was Göring's mandate to Heydrich, given after Kristallnacht, to form a Reich Central Office for Jewish Emigration in Berlin, that decisively elevated Heydrich and his staff to leading players in the Jewish question. It was this mandate, in fact, or rather its extension in July 1941, that Heydrich used as the formal legitimation to call the Wannsee conference.[26]

Why did so many groups and individuals take up the war against the Jews with such enthusiasm? Historians have been understandably reluctant to believe that educated, competent bureaucrats should be driven by something as irrational as anti-Semitism. One unbalanced individual might hold such an obsession, but could an entire class of educated men? Surely, their objectives would be more grounded in material interests? Certainly, in a system where an official ideology was at the heart of the revolutionary movement's claim to rule, ideology itself became a strategic tool in the exercise and pursuit of power. Anti-Semitism was the badge ambitious individuals could wear to legitimate their claims and demands. Many players in the game might be hard put to identify how far they truly subscribed to anti-Semitic beliefs and how far anti-Semitism was deployed instrumentally in pursuit of power.

But recent research has begun to rediscover the power of anti-Semitism as a guiding principle, less for the German population as a whole than for an important and influential minority within German society. After all, in the early 1920s the Nazi Party was merely one of a horde of small groups on the radical right advocating similar brands of ideology. Far from being distinctive, the Party's ethnic nationalism and virulent anti-Semitism was the common currency of the radical right and continued to be so throughout the 1920s. Between 1930 and 1933 the Party muted its public anti-Semitism, but the ideology continued to be vital for internal consumption, and survived in Party propaganda in both overt and coded form.[27] The local uprising against Jewish businesses that gathered momentum as soon as the regime came to power demonstrated a 'sincere' and strongly felt agenda at all levels of the Party.[28]

Among the conservative elites, too, there is little doubt that the goal of excluding Jews from positions of power, reducing their influence in cultural life and limiting their numbers in the population, was widely shared. On these matters, Hitler could count on enthusiastic co-operation from sufficient sections of army, civil service and other influential areas of society to create a powerful climate for change. It was striking, for example, that, even after his dismissal by the Nazis on trumped-up grounds in 1938, the conservative General Werner Freiherr von Fritsch could still write in a private letter that the battle against the Jews was one of the most important and most difficult tasks of National Socialism.[29] Alongside anti-Semitism, another point of overlap between Nazis and conservative elites was widespread toleration of violence, the result of Germany's experience of defeat and of internal civil war in the 1920s. As Bernd Weisbrod has shown, there was striking tacit acceptance of violence among bourgeois groups whom one might have expected to disdain such behaviour.[30] The tolerance of Hitler's murderous Night of the Long Knives in 1934, a night of terror which cost the lives of over 100 people, including the former chancellor, General Kurt von Schleicher, and his wife, is ample evidence of this.

Highly significant too was the sizeable minority among the edu-cated members of the so-called war youth generation (born from the turn of the century to 1910 or so) who most strongly bought into the ideas of the radical right. Far more than society as a whole, the student body of the 1920s reacted to war, defeat, Germany's international humiliation and the massive economic difficulties of the time by endorsing radical racially anti-Semitic and ethnic-nationalist ideas. The radical right-wing Deutscher Hochschulring won more than two thirds of seats in student parliaments in the early 1920s. In 1926 77 per cent of Prussian students voted to keep Jews out of the association.[31] Thus, a substantial group within this cohort were persuaded of the values of *völkisch* nationalism. The perceived injustice of the post-Versailles world order proved to them the arbitrariness of international rules of law and citizenship. The Weimar state and constitution were rejected long before Hitler came to power.[32] Hitler answered the desire for a new ethnic politics and for a powerful state, capable of dealing with internal and external enemies.

Until 1935–6 the most obvious forms of anti-Semitism in the Third Reich were the vulgar, thuggish outbursts of the Party and the restrained antipathy of the conservative bureaucracy. Hitler mediated between and manipulated both strands. With the expansion of the SD and the security police a new kind of anti-Semitic grouping emerged – as fanatic and committed as the Party rank and file, but hostile to street violence, seeking a rational and organized solution. 'If there was ever a central group responsible for the National Socialist policies of genocide and persecution', as Ulrich Herbert has written recently, it was the 300 or so men who made up the leadership of the security services within Heydrich's RSHA. These men would be the guiding spirits in the Einsatzkommandos and the security police in occupied Europe in the early 1940s.[33]

Heydrich's staff were extraordinarily youthful: in 1939 two thirds of those in leadership positions were aged thirty-six or under.[34] Since they were also highly educated, they exemplified the characteristics of the student cohort we mentioned earlier. Their racist-nationalist values were all the more destructive because they were often not felt to be an ideology at all. Many of the younger men regarded themselves as realists, inured to the flowery rhetoric of older Nazis such as Himmler, Alfred Rosenberg or Walter Darré.[35] They advocated a modern rational 'Realpolitik', or in Werner Best's words 'Heroic Realism', by which law and the normal proprieties should be subordinated to the ruthless pursuit of national power.[36] It is probable that without Hitler's leadership anti-Semitism would not have figured quite so prominently in this group's concerns.[37] Even in the late 1930s, the SS newspaper *Das Schwarze Korps* was as obsessed with political Catholicism as with Jewish matters.[38] But once it responded to Hitler's agenda, this cohort, with its shared philosophy of racial struggle and its style of unflinching warrior, had the will to carry it forward.

Signposts

The shared agenda of Hitler, Party, state and SS in the 1930s was to reduce Jewish influence and encourage Jewish emigration, not to carry out mass murder. Yet the road the Nazis travelled was littered with signposts that point more directly towards Wannsee. For one thing, the approach to emigration was contradictory.[39] Fears of a Jewish world conspiracy led the Nazis to hamper Jews' freedom to emigrate, not least by restricting the destinations they might choose.[40] Above all, the progressive impoverishment of potential emigrants and the increasingly draconian export restrictions for capital and currency made it hard for Jews to leave and disinclined other countries from accepting them.[41] Yet Hitler made repeated warnings that, if current measures did not deal with the Jews, worse would follow.[42] Towards the end of the 1930s he began to air the idea of some kind of reservation for the Jews not just of Germany but of the rest of Europe. In September 1938 he told the Polish ambassador Jozef Lipski he hoped to settle the Jewish question by mutual agreement with Poland, Hungary and Romania. He was thinking of shipping the Jews to a colony. Lipski replied that if Hitler could find a solution to the problem the Poles would build a monument in his honour. In January 1939 Hitler discussed the problem at length in meetings with eastern European leaders, indicating to the Polish Minister of Foreign Affairs, Jozef Beck, that he favoured settling the Jews in a distant land. He added that if the western powers had allowed him he might have placed an African colony at their disposal.[43]

These pronouncements reflected Hitler's belief that an international Jewish conspiracy was manipulating world events. As his foreign policy grew increasingly radical and the rest of the world correspondingly suspicious, so Hitler grew more threatening towards the Jews. As early as 1931 he had warned that if it came to a new war the Jews would be 'crushed by the wheels of history'.[44] In October 1935 the Berlin journal *Judenkenner* threatened, 'If a foreign army, under orders of the Jews, should ever enter German territory then it will have to march over the corpses of slain Hebrews.'[45] In the late 1930s the warnings grew more urgent. Most infamous of all, in a speech to the Reichstag on 30 January 1939, Hitler 'wished to make a prophecy: if international Jewry in and outside Europe once again forced the nations into a world war the result would not be the Bolshevization of the earth and victory for the Jews but the annihilation of the Jewish race in Europe'.[46]

Hitler's threats and prophecies were partly blackmail. If international Jewry was manipulating world affairs, then Germany's Jews might be used as hostages to tame their brethren abroad.[47] We should not treat literally Hitler's comments to foreign statesmen about creating a Jewish reservation. Hitler was sending out warnings. Even so, his prophecies were not merely tactical gestures. He believed the Jews were not only manipulating the world powers against Germany, but also formed an internationalist fifth column seeking to undermine Germany from within. Germany's defeat in the First World War had been the result of these diabolical machinations. This fifth column therefore had to be removed. More generally still, Hitler saw war offering opportunities for radical social engineering. If post-war testimony is to be believed, he said in 1935, for example, that once war came he would institute compulsory euthanasia for the handicapped. Murders of those with mental and physical disabilities did indeed begin soon after the outbreak of hostilities.[48]

As the risk of war loomed, the rhetoric grew still more lethal. In November 1938 Himmler predicted that there would be a battle between Germans and Jews. The Jews would be merciless if they won, bringing total starvation and massacre to Germany. The corollary was clear but not spelled out. On 24 November 1938 *Das Schwarze Korps* said that Jews could not continue to live in Germany. 'This stage of development will impose on us the vital necessity to exterminate this Jewish sub-humanity, as we exterminate all criminals in our ordered country: by the fire and the sword! The outcome will be the final catastrophe for Jewry in Germany, its total annihilation.'[49]

Deportations to nowhere

In the longer view, the outbreak of war was the decisive event in unleashing the Nazis' full murderous potential. Yet when the assault on Poland began in September 1939 Nazi thinking was still a long way from genocide.[50] Indeed, until as late as summer 1941, the regime continued to promote Jewish emigration. It would be more than two years from the start of the war before the Nazis fully embraced mass murder.

From the outset, war did, none the less, force a rethink. The scope for Jewish emigration had been significantly reduced by the closure of British and Commonwealth territories to German refugees, but as Poland fell into German hands, the Nazis acquired a new 'Jewish problem' – well over two million additional Jews under their control. What was to be done with them?

The answer emerged very rapidly, though the details shifted a little over the following weeks, in the context of radical plans for Poland. Poland's western provinces (large parts of which had been Prussian before 1918) were to be annexed to the German Reich. Many of the Polish citizens there would be expelled to a rump Polish area under German administration, the Generalgouvernement. In the eastern part of the Generalgouvernement, between the Vistula and Bug rivers, there would be a reservation for the Jews. Here, the Jews of Poland and greater Germany could be deposited.

Given that there had been little or no advance planning, the speed with which Heydrich's staff now set to work was breathtaking.

Within three weeks of the outbreak of war Heydrich announced to his staff that Jews could be deported into the Generalgouvernement and that they could also be shoved across the partition into the Russian-held areas of the country.[51] Heydrich's subordinate, Adolf Eichmann, the RSHA official for Jewish affairs, readied himself for an advance programme of deportations involving some 75,000 Jews. Yet just as striking as the speed with which the programme had begun was the fact that it collapsed almost as quickly. Indeed, up to summer 1941 only a few thousand German Jews were dispatched to Poland from German-held territories. Even from the annexed Polish territories, now the Wartheland and West Prussia, supposed to be cleared of their former non-German inhabitants, deportations of Jews were far more limited than planned and only a fraction of the far more substantial non-Jewish Polish deportations.[52]

The priority accorded the matter was undoubted. Why had the Germans not achieved more? The army managed to ring-fence some scarce rail resources. But above all it was because of another gigantic resettlement programme which Himmler, now appointed Reich Commissar for the Strengthening of Germandom, unfurled in the 1939–40 period. The regime entered into a series of agreements with foreign powers to resettle ethnic Germans living abroad and bring them 'home'. Its favoured destination to settle these lost sheep was West Prussia and the Wartheland. Polish farmers living in these areas were to be expropriated, their farmsteads handed over to the immigrants and the farmers themselves shoved over the border into the Generalgouvernement. Although some thousands of Polish Jews were included in this process, the scope specifically for Jewish resettlement, and above all for deportation of Jews from elsewhere in Germany into Poland, was now extremely limited.

The officials in the receiving areas also began to revolt. Restive at administering a social 'refuse tip', the Generalgouvernement's Governor, Hans Frank, aspired to create a model colony. A model colony required not the settlement but the expulsion of Jews, partly for prestige and racial reasons and partly because Frank's economic experts told him that the region was overpopulated. Frank vigorously lobbied for a stop to deportations. When Göring added his backing, concerned about the economic implications of uncontrolled population movements, the idea of using Poland as a dumping ground very rapidly ran out of steam. On 12 March 1940 Hitler declared the Jewish Question was one of space and that he had none at his disposal. Thus by 15 November 1940 just 5,000 Jews from Prague, Vienna and Mährisch-Ostrau, 1,000 from Stettin and 2,800 gypsies had been deported.[53]

If Poland could not absorb Germany's Jews, and its own were unwanted, where to with them? The most significant development was the fantastical interlude during which Madagascar was proposed as an alternative area of settlement. First raised in the 1930s, the idea was mooted by Himmler in May 1940. This led to an initiative by Fritz Rademacher from the Foreign Office. Having made some initial investigations in this direction in the 1930s, the RSHA rushed to come up with its own plan. In June Hitler gave Admiral Erich Raeder and Benito Mussolini to understand that he believed Madagascar could seriously be a colony for the Jews. Eichmann's assistants went on tropical training courses and received inoculations against malaria. In Poland Hans Frank too took the idea very seriously, seeing it as an opportunity to empty Poland of Jews. But by August it was clear that the absence of naval victory over Britain made such plans untenable.[54]

As late as spring 1941, on the eve of Operation Barbarossa, the Nazis were still committed to finding a territory to which to deport Europe's Jews.[55] It fits into the story of improvisation and lack of clear planning but is nevertheless still astonishing that a major territorial policy had been improvised in a few weeks in September–October 1939, had run aground after just a few weeks more, and then in effect marked time for eighteen months.

Occupied with murder

If by spring 1941 Nazi policy was incomparably closer to the territory of the Wannsee conference than it had been in September 1939, it was not because genocide had yet entered the agenda. It was rather that under the aegis of war and occupation Nazi governance and social engineering had taken on almost unimaginable brutality. The concept of a Jewish reservation was in two senses very different from that of emigration (though support for emigration continued). The function of a reservation, at least as the Nazis imagined it, was to provide an unpropitious, punishing environment in which the Jewish race would fail to thrive. Eichmann's staff worked deliberately to select the most unhealthy areas. No one put this aspect of the programme more brutally than Governor Frank: 'A pleasure finally to physically assault the Jewish race. The more die, the better (...) The Jews should notice that we have arrived. We want half or three quarters of them east of the Vistula.'[56] Moreover it evinced a gigantic new scale to Nazi social engineering. The plans on Himmler's drawing-board involved truly massive population transfers that would reshape the ethnic mix of the whole of eastern Europe. Himmler's agenda was far from purely anti-Jewish, indeed policy towards Jews was stymied by the wider consideration of ethnic German resettlement. But blueprints on this scale rendered conceivable what had previously been beyond imagining. As Himmler's resettlement apparatus extended its influence into all levels of the Polish administration, it created new pressures for action.[57]

Equally important, and here Hitler's imprint was evident, the grand design was not accompanied by commensurate careful planning. Commitments were entered into and timetables drawn up with heedless speed. Transports were dispatched hither and thither with no thought for the consequences. Even the ethnic Germans were shoved around Europe without proper calculation. By the winter of 1940/41 ¼ million of the returnees were still sitting in 1,500 reception camps waiting for resettlement. But their suffering was as nought compared with that of the hundreds of thousands of Poles and Jews uprooted from their homes and dumped in the Generalgouvernement. On a 1940 round-up of German Jews from Stettin, for example, 1,200 people, many of them elderly, were dumped at night in Poland and sent on a twenty-kilometre march along snow-covered roads. Many hundreds died from their exertions. Beyond driving the victims from the train, no thought had been wasted on their fate.[58]

As well as triggering these massive resettlements, war brought about another significant change. Hitler had always regarded murder as a legitimate means of political struggle. Occupation provided the stimulus and opportunity to deploy it much more extensively as a tool of political control and social engineering. In August 1939 Hitler decided, as Heydrich put it to his subordinates on 7 September, that 'the social elite in Poland' should 'as far as possible be rendered harmless'.[59] Heydrich established so-called Einsatzkommandos comprising security police (SiPo), SD, ordinary police and the militarized (Waffen) SS. These men moved in behind the Wehrmacht to deal with the enemies of the Reich. From the last third of October 1939 mass executions began, targeting among others, teachers, academics, officers, civil servants, priests and the mentally ill. Among them were many Jews: of 16,000 civilians killed in the six weeks following the attack, 5,000 were Jewish and by the end of the year probably 7,000 Jews had been killed. The operation was not primarily designed as a solution to the Jewish question, rather as the elimination of potential Polish national leadership. But the addictive habit of killing was being acquired.[60]

Murder was deployed as a surgical technique of social control in a very different context. Just prior to the outbreak of war Hitler had authorized the creation of a special programme to select and eliminate physically or mentally handicapped children who would be a burden on the state. Even before the policy began to be implemented, it was extended to handicapped adults. Here again, the Polish and ex-Polish territories provided the research laboratory. From December 1939 the inmates of psychiatric hospitals were murdered in the Warthegau. Gas was used for the first time as an instrument of murder. In general, the murder of the mentally ill was an important link in the chain to the later killing of Jews. Some time in spring 1940 the euthanasia squads began to murder all Jews with mental health problems without subjecting them to the same tests that were applied (albeit often arbitrarily) elsewhere. In summer 1940, in preparation for the abortive Madagascar deportations, all mentally ill Jews in psychiatric institutions were murdered. It would still take major psychological steps to move from eliminating those deemed 'unworthy of life' to killing all Jews. Nevertheless, the departments and staffs involved in administering the euthanasia programme would later be devoting their energy and expertise to exterminating Jews.[61]

Beyond these examples, the Polish arena gave free rein to a more diffuse climate of brutality and murderousness, already evident in miniature in the 1930s. Again, Hitler set the tone. At a meeting with army leaders on 22 August 1939, one of those present made shorthand notes of Hitler's language. 'The Destruction of Poland. The Goal is the elimination of the living forces, not reaching a particular line. Close one's heart to sympathy. Brutal approach.' A clear indication of his central role can be seen in the evolving relationship between Hitler, the army and ordinary soldiers. In the first weeks of the Polish occupation much of the violence against Jews came not from Heydrich's special squads but from ordinary soldiers, whose anti-Semitism was aroused by the strange-looking eastern Jews. Though the soldiers will, of course, have been influenced by the climate of anti-Semitism long propagated by the Nazi leadership, this was not centrally ordered. Some officers, it is true, took part in the brutal dispatching of Jews across the Soviet demarcation line. Senior army figures, however, grew increasingly concerned at such excesses and sought both to rein in their own troops and to curb the behaviour of the Einsatzgruppen. This was the last moment when the tone might have been set for a more conventional kind of occupation and for a more restrained kind of war. Hitler's response was to offer an amnesty for all those who had committed excesses, to remove the army's responsibility for the administration of Poland and to end the military courts' jurisdiction over the SS and Einsatzgruppen. Even those generals who, like Colonel-General Georg von Küchler, had fiercely objected to the crimes, now fell into line. Within a little more than a year and a half the army would be docile participants in genocide.[62]

Whereas in the Reich the Nazis had had to interact with existing elites, the administrations in the east were staffed with their own. The SD and security police officials in particular were almost all long-time Nazis. Hostility to Poles and particularly to Jews was the common currency of administration attitudes. In this climate, the pogrom-style violence of the Party man, the controlled brutality of the security police and the callous disregard for local interests of the 'colonial' civil servant began to meld. Once the deportations ran aground, Berlin's interest in the treatment of Jews in Poland declined and the men at the lower level were given greater freedom to get on with it. Local measures were sufficiently divergent to prove there was no coherent murder plan. But actions in Warsaw, Lublin and elsewhere were sufficiently lethal to give rise to a quite widely held belief among well-informed observers in Poland that after the war the Jews would be eliminated altogether.[63]

Stalemate and frustration

Within the German administration in Poland the general assumption in summer 1940 or even spring 1941 was not that there would be a post-war extermination. Rather it was the conviction that the Jews had to leave the region. Governor Frank rejected the idea of the Polish dumping ground. In the course of 1939–40 a series of ideas emerged about rational use of Polish land resources for the good of Germany – either under direct German settlement or as provider of resources for the German nation. By the summer of 1940 it was common currency among Frank's staff that the Jews and at least some of the non-Jewish Poles had to go, in order to make the area economically efficient. The more pressure placed on the region to provide surplus food for the Reich, the more the civilian administration sought to transfer 'surplus' population further east.[64]

At the same time, back home within the Reich, frustration grew at all levels with the slow pace of Jewish expulsions. In Vienna complaints about the continued presence of Jews could be heard from a variety of local Party figures almost as soon as the war began. In December 1940 the Viennese gauleiter, Baldur von Schirach, added his voice to the clamour. Hitler promised support, though the eventual expulsions were again very limited in number. In spring 1941 it was Goebbels's turn to complain; he too was told no deportations could take place at present. Above all, Heydrich and Eichmann nailed their institutional colours and prestige to the goal of clearing the Reich of Jews. When Eichmann received orders to desist after the first wave of Jewish deportations to the Generalgouvernement, for example, he insisted that one further transport be dispatched 'to maintain the prestige of the state police'.[65] It was a major provocation for the RSHA that every attempt to expel Jews ended in failure. Territorial solutions continued to be the official goal, but there was a growing sense of grimness about the need to get the task sorted.[66] Hitler was bombarded with requests for more action.

Genocidal war begins

Occupied Poland in 1940 to 1941 bubbled over with acts of brutality. In the little town of Izbica the new ethnic-German mayor trained his dog to recognize the Jewish star. Women on the way to the well for water were brought down by the mayor's beloved Alsatian and murdered for sport. In Odilo Globocnik's labour camps Jews constructing defensive fortifications along the Bug river died in droves. Games were played by the guards making them leap from truck to truck on moving goods trains. Such examples go into the thousands and tens of thousands and there is already an authentic Holocaust flavour here. And yet at the level of high planning with which we are concerned, genocide had still not entered the agenda. It was the war against the Soviet Union that was to make the decisive difference.

On 22 June 1941 German troops entered Soviet territory. Behind the troops swept in four motorized Einsatzgruppen of 600 to 1,000 men each. Karl Jäger, the head of one of the sub-commandos operating within the northern group, Einsatzgruppe A, reported in December on the activities of his own unit, Einsatzkommando 3:

I can now state that the aim of solving the Jewish problem for Lithuania has been achieved by Einsatzkommando 3. There are no more Jews in Lithuania apart from the work-Jews and their families . . .

The carrying out of such actions is first and foremost a matter of organiz- ation. The decision to clear each district systematically of Jews required a thorough preparation of every single action and the investigation of the conditions in the particular district. The Jews had to be concentrated in one place or in several places. The place for the pits which were required had to be found and dug out to suit the numbers involved. The distance from the place where the Jews were concentrated to the pits was on average 4–5km. The Jews were transported to the place of execution in groups of up to 500 with gaps of at least 2km . . .[67]

By the time of his report, mass shootings by Einsatzkommandos and other killing units had led to the deaths of half a million Jews. The Nazis had entered the era of genocide.

This was not an ordinary war, Hitler told his generals, but a fight to the death between two ideologies. The Soviet state had to be destroyed through the most brutal violence. The Communist officials were all criminals and must be treated as such.[68] The latter demand was perhaps not so different from his instruction of August 1939 that the Polish leadership be eliminated. The disastrous difference as far as Jews were concerned was that Hitler believed Jews were at the heart of the Communist system. Hitler's aim was the elimination of the 'Judeo-Bolshevik intelligentsia'. In Russia, therefore, the cam- paign against the elites was to be from the beginning also a campaign against the Jews, with the limits of the Jewish culpability and partici- pation very poorly defined.

Hitler could count on the enthusiastic endorsement of the security police. The planning for the tasks of the four Einsatzgruppen sent into the Soviet Union was undertaken by Reinhard Heydrich in the months before Barbarossa. The same highly educated elite that staffed the SD's think-tank now provided the cool commanders of the Einsatz squads. The detailed headcounts sent back to Berlin, listing carefully and separately the Jewish men, women and children shot during the reporting period, reveal for the first time in its full horror the unique fusion of annihilatory ideology and bureaucratic pernicketiness that now characterized Heydrich's staff. Striking too was the degree to which the army now accepted anti-Jewish measures as an essential part of the fight against the Soviet leadership. Sharing Hitler's anti-Bolshevism and anti-Semitism and having learned subservience in Poland, the Army High Command willingly planned a new kind of war.[69] The infamous *Kommissarbefehl* of 6 June laid down that all political commissars attached to the Red Army should be shot.[70] The army accepted that the SS would have 'special tasks' within its zone of operation, and that it was entitled to act against the civilian population on its own authority. For both army and Einsatzkommandos, anti-Bolshevism and anti-partisan actions became the legitimation for action against Jewish civilians.[71]

The Soviet war was predicated on murder in another sense too. As a number of historians have emphasized recently, Hitler's *va banque* military strategy, and indeed his longer-term settlement plans, depended on ruthless commandeering of Soviet resources, above all its foodstuffs.[72] On 2 May 1941 the Reich's economic experts concluded that war could be sustained beyond the end of the year only if German soldiers on Russian soil were fed from Russian supplies. The dry conclusion was that 'Doubtless tens of millions [*Zigmillionen*] of people will starve to death.'[73] The German High Command deliberately made no provision to feed the expected millions of Soviet prisoners. The result was an astonishingly high death toll among the POWs – initially far higher than the number of Jews who were killed. Over the summer pressures on food resources grew because of failure to make sufficient military advance and because it became clear that the fields had not been properly planted. There was a growing clamour to eliminate 'useless eaters'.[74] From September the rations for POWs were lowered still further and by the end of 1941 a staggering *two million* Soviet prisoners had died in German hands.[75] This murderous (non-)planning shows that millions of deaths off the battlefield were a calculated and integral part of the campaign.

Barbarossa, then, created murderous imperatives and altered the whole tone of the war. But did this mean that there was from the beginning a clear decision to murder all Soviet Jews, or a more limited strategic concept (eliminating the Judeo-Bolshevik intelligentsia) that later widened into something more comprehensive? Unfortunately, a lot of Heydrich's planning is concealed from us. We know far less about the instructions given to the Einsatzgruppen commanders than we do about the Wehrmacht's basic directives. Preserved is only a précis of Heydrich's instructions handed on in June to Himmler's direct subordinates in the field, the higher SS and police leaders in the Soviet Union.[76] This document indicates that 'all Jews in the service of Party and state' should be targeted, an instruction not intrinsically genocidal, though only very vaguely delimited. It seems quite possible that Heydrich's verbal instructions to the Einsatzgruppen went beyond the written orders.[77]

If we look at the actual practice of the killing squads, we can see that by and large they began by targeting a narrower group of state officials and Jews in leading positions but widened their remit very rapidly to include all Jewish men of military age.[78] A few weeks later in July–August, women and children began to be included and in August–September squads moved to eliminate entire communities systematically.[79] Was this the step-wise implementation of a pre-existing plan or did the instructions change over the summer? If so, who ordered the widening of the killing? Post-war trial testimony of captured Einsatzgruppen and -kommando leaders is extremely contradictory, as are their progress reports submitted during the war.[80] The reports, while confirming the general trend to greater comprehensiveness, also indicate considerable variations in local commanders' interpretations of their brief. As early as July 1941 the leader of Einsatzgruppe A believed that the special conditions in the Soviet Union made possible the murder of all Jews.[81] Yet even in

September Einsatzgruppe C did not seem to think that eliminating Jews was its principal task.[82]

Whatever instructions the group and local commanders had initially received, therefore, had been susceptible to narrower or broader interpretation. This suggests that the initial orders were not clearly genocidal, but that a loose definition of the Jewish elite was deployed which allowed for something quite close to genocide – namely the elimination of all Jewish men of working age. Once killings on that scale had been carried out, it often seemed but a small step to widen the scope of murder. The widows and children of the murdered men did not look like a 'viable' community, particularly in view of the intensifying food shortages.

Hitler certainly set the general climate for this radicalization of policy. We know that he asked for regular reports on the Einsatz-gruppen activities. A shooting may even have been filmed for him.[83] More generally, at an important meeting on 16 July following which he gave Rosenberg jurisdiction over those areas not still directly under military command, Hitler said that Germany would never leave the conquered territories. All measures necessary for a final settlement – such as shooting and deportation – should be taken. Stalin's partisan war provided the excuse to 'exterminate anything opposing us' – 'anyone who even looks at us the wrong way should be shot'.[84] These statements were made in confident anticipation of rapid victory. Towards the end of July, however, it became apparent that progress was slower than expected, and that supplying the troops was causing major problems. Now it was Göring's turn to send some harsh signals down. On 27/28 July he ordered that all food production in the occupied eastern territories should be centrally controlled and allocated only to those who worked for Germany. The civilian administration had already begun to distinguish between Jews and non-Jews; Göring now extended this discrimination to the whole of the occupied Soviet Union.[85]

It was above all Himmler who conveyed the need for more radical measures. On 17 July 1941 Hitler placed security in the civilian regions in the east in Himmler's hands. From 15 to 20 July Himmler was in the Führer's headquarters. We do not know what communication he had with Hitler but, whatever took place, Himmler rapidly moved from policies that still might be characterized as murderous security measures to ones that could only be seen as genocidal – solving the 'Jewish problem' in large areas of the conquered Soviet Union by killing. Himmler was acting here not only with his security mandate from Hitler, but also in seeking informally (later officially) to extend his role as Reich Commissar for the Strengthening of Germandom from Poland to the former Soviet territories. Within a week of his appointment Himmler quadrupled the number of SS men operating behind army lines. That was just the beginning, since Himmler now assigned the police reserve battalions to the higher SS and police leaders (HSSPF). Through the HSSPF, Himmler began to press for the radical cleansing of huge swathes of territory for both security and settlement objectives. There was at the end of July perhaps a little hesitation still at ordering the killings of women and children, but only a little.[86] Increasingly, the HSSPF took on the leading role in the killing process, and the SS-brigades and police battalions under their direction eventually murdered far more Jews than the original Einsatzgruppen.[87]

Overall, the evidence does not support the idea that there was one single clear-cut order to murder all Jews. The point in time at which the individual Einsatzgruppen widened the scope of their killing varied considerably. What we can say is that in a general murderous climate fostered by Hitler, a variety of agencies worked together rapidly to push measures forward, with the Himmler–Heydrich axis at the centre. The Einsatzgruppen leaders themselves, most of them stemming from the educated, ideologically homogenous security police ambit that we have already described, liberally interpreted their brief. In the latter half of July and first half of August Himmler, perhaps under instructions from Hitler, moved towards a more openly genocidal line. As economic pressures increased, the SS-security police leadership found further encouragement from civilian officials complaining about undesirable elements making claims on scarce resources. The civilian administration in Lithuania and some field commanders in the Wehrmacht drew up agreements with the SS to get rid of the 'useless eaters' left behind by the first shootings. By August 1941 at the latest, the fate of Soviet Jewry was sealed.[88]

3

Mass murder to genocide

The elusive Hitler decision

The few weeks following the outbreak of war against the Soviet Union had changed the climate irrevocably. Assumptions about what was feasible, inhibitions about what was intolerable were discarded and remoulded in interaction with events. As early as July Himmler's thoughts turned to experimenting with gas as an alternative to shooting. At the same time knowledge of the shootings spread among Nazi elites in Germany and elsewhere in occupied Europe. Their own perception of what was possible began to change too. Some psychological threshold was irrevocably crossed.

Yet it was still a major step from murdering indiscriminately in the lawless conditions behind the military front line to the project expressed in the Wannsee Protocol of systematically extracting and murdering Jews all across Europe. How and when was this transition effected? The simple answer, which has not always been voiced as openly as it might have been, is that our need for precise answers is greater than the ability of the documentation to supply them. Most historians continue to assume that, however twisted the road may have been to reach this point, in such a Hitler-centred system Hitler must still at some point have taken the ultimate decision. His role in redefining the character of warfare and introducing murderous pacification and social engineering had been crucial. But how closely did he now direct the killing of Jews? Was his approval given or merely presumed? Did the transition from mass killings to genocide indeed involve a clear decision, or was the kind of programme outlined at Wannsee more of a retrospective codification of a process already under way?

Even more than in peacetime, Hitler carefully concealed his involvement in the Jewish question.[1] The paucity of official records is not compensated by the existence of private ones. Hitler kept no diary and sent no letters expressing views on the Jewish question. A number of those close to him recorded his views, but often the notes of Hitler's subordinates are ambiguous too. We are then faced with the challenge not only of understanding what Nazi leaders *thought* Hitler had said but also of ascertaining whether they got it right. In any case, we have virtually no record of probably the most important channel of communication on the Jewish question, Hitler's conversations with Himmler. The occasional entries in Himmler's appointments diary regarding Hitler and the Jewish question are abbreviated and cryptic.

The statements we do have on record from Hitler are forthright enough, but Hitler's rhetoric as we have seen is so inflammatory. There is a relationship between his brutal words and brutal policies but it is not a direct one. Take the issue of Hitler's 'prophecy' of January 1939 that a future world war would lead to the extermination of Jews in Europe. There is no doubt that this warning was significant, not least in establishing the rhetorical climate for his subordinates. For some historians, it represented the clear threat of physical genocide. Yet there is no evidence that mass extermination was being planned in 1939. Hitler himself made little reference to the prophecy throughout the whole of 1940. So we are not sure if the statements themselves are evidence of clear intent or, indeed, *if* clear, precisely what the intent was. Hitler's warning was that annihilation would follow if the Jews should plunge Europe into *world* war. Is it possible that he did not yet see the conflict with Britain and the Commonwealth as world war? Something that might support such an idea is that in January 1941, when war with the Soviet Union was in the offing, Hitler recalled his prophecy of two years earlier and thereafter returned to it more often. Yet his timing then may have been a response to other developments that were changing his thinking rather than reveal a consistent understanding of what 'world war' meant.

It is also uncertain if the 'annihilation' of Jews in Europe implied a clearly formulated desire for their physical deaths rather than complete removal of their presence and culture from within its borders. Hitler repeatedly talked of the need to drive the Jews out of Germany by force. Brutal means were required to cleanse the racial state. But his pronouncements seldom unequivocally crossed the line from physical removal to physical extermination.

The dominant impression from Hitler's table talk is not the clear goal-setting of the policy-maker but the late-night ramblings of an ignoramus at a *Bier Keller*. The thought that the speaker was presiding over the fate of million of lives is almost inconceivable. With monologues as rambling as this, how could even his closest confidants know what his intentions were? Were the issue not genocide, of course, Hitler's responsibility would be beyond question. We would not be interrogating his language so relentlessly and would accept almost any of his statements as proof of his intentions. But the Holocaust is so murderously innovative that we want to understand precisely how the taboos could be broken.

Extending killings: July 1941

Until recently most historians would have chosen one or other of two moments as the most likely point at which Hitler committed himself to eliminating European Jewry. One was sometime in mid-July, just before Himmler moved to extend the killings in the Soviet Union, the other in mid-September, when Hitler approved the deportation of German Jews eastwards.

In mid-July, anticipating imminent victory over the Soviet Union, Hitler took some fundamental policy decisions, laying down brutal guidelines for the 'pacification' and colonization of Soviet territory. It was in the wake of these decisions that Himmler radically extended the killings in the Soviet Union. Goebbels wrote in his diary at the beginning of August that 'The Führer is convinced that his former prophecy in the Reichstag is being confirmed: if Jewry succeeded once in provoking a world war, it would end with the annihilation of the Jews. It is being confirmed in these weeks and months with a certainty that seems almost uncanny.'[2] The commandant of Auschwitz, Rudolf Höβ, stated after the war that he was summoned to Himmler in summer 1941 and told that Auschwitz was going to be an extermination centre for the Jews. During his trial in Jerusalem, Adolf Eichmann too said he learned in summer 1941 about a fundamental Hitler decision. We think that around this time Himmler began thinking of using gas as an alternative to shooting.[3] Friedrich Suhr, jurist in the RSHA, was now officially designated 'Official for the Final Solution of the European Jewish Question, particularly abroad'. On 28 July 1941 Viktor Brack, the man in charge of the T4 (euthanasia) operation, asked for support from the military economic administration for a major forthcoming action. As far as we know, no forthcoming operation was planned within the euthanasia programme as such.

Above all, there is Göring's infamous *Ermächtigung* (authorization) to Heydrich of 31 July 1941, which many historians have seen as the authentic inception of genocide:

In completion of the task entrusted to you in the edict dated January 24th 1939 of solving the Jewish question by means of migration or evacuation in the most convenient way possible, given the present conditions, I herewith charge you with making all necessary preparations with regard to organizational, practical and financial aspects for an overall solution of the Jewish question in the German sphere of influence in Europe.

Insofar as the competencies of other central organization are affected, these should be involved.

I further charge you with submitting to me promptly an overall plan of the preliminary organizational, practical and financial measures for the execution of the intended final solution of the Jewish question.[4]

Yet thanks to recent research in the former Soviet archives we now know a little more about the background to the Göring document.

Heydrich himself produced the first draft of the authorization as early as March 1941, noting at the time that he had submitted it to Göring for signature but that agreement with Rosenberg was required before it could be authorized.[5] Rosenberg was the minister-designate for the occupied Soviet territories and it looks as if Heydrich was seeking Göring's approval to develop a new deportation policy into Siberia or some other eastern Soviet territory, now that the Polish deportations had failed. It is known that from the end of 1940 to early 1941 preparations were being made for large-scale future deportation of all Jews under German influence to some eastern area.[6] Discussions in the interim then clarified Rosenberg's role, enabling Heydrich to re-present the earlier draft in July.[7] Of course, the terms in the authorization – 'overall solution' (*Gesamtlösung*) and 'final solution' (*Endlösung*) of the Jewish question – were soon to be euphemisms for murder. By the end of November, when Heydrich attached this document to the invitations to the Wannsee conference as proof of his authority, there is little doubt that 'final solution' had lost any other meaning. But up to 1941 Heydrich for one regularly distinguished between 'interim' and 'final' solutions without meaning genocide – for example in relation to the Czech question.[8] We do not need to assume that the terms had attained their clear code meaning by July.

The other evidence for a July decision for genocide also begins to lose its persuasiveness. Both Höβ's and Eichmann's testimonies lack credibility. The evidence is overwhelming that Höβ's meeting with Himmler took place at least nine months later than he remembered.[9] Above all, Höβ made clear that the point at which he learned about Auschwitz's new function was when the extermination camps in Poland were already functioning – and that can have been only in 1942.[10] Eichmann was at pains to establish a clear set of orders that removed his own responsibility. In interviews given in freedom in Argentina and in his first interrogation, he said that he learned about the final solution only at the end of 1941. But later he claimed that he heard of Hitler's order in summer 1941. However, the details he attached to the memory, relating to a visit to the Bełżec camp, meant that it cannot have happened before November 1941.[11]

What we find in spring and summer 1941, in fact, is growing clamour from different groups hoping to use the Soviet territory as a dumping ground for German and other European Jews. Hitler himself made various pronouncements about the deportation of Europe's Jews. Before the start of the Russian campaign he had promised Hans Frank, Governor of the Polish Generalgouvernement, that the Jews would be removed from there in the foreseeable future.[12] On 22 July he announced to the Croatian Marshal Slavko Kvaternik his intention to deport Jews, saying it was a matter of indifference to him whether they were sent to Madagascar or Siberia.[13] Whether his use of the language of deportation was sincere or not, other Nazi officials certainly drew the conclusion from conversations with Hitler that European Jews were going to be sent to the east. Having already made initiatives in March to send Jews to the Generalgouvernement and failed, Goebbels noted delightedly in June that they were all looking forward to expelling their Jews. For Hans Frank Russia represented the answer to his prayers.[14]

Nagging doubts must remain. Did the Germans really want to deport Jews to the Soviet Union, when even after a successful war they expected border skirmishes to continue for some time? Were they likely to deposit the arch-enemy, the Jews, in an area where they could gain contact with Germany's enemies? Possibly, if the borders were suitably policed.[15] What is certain is that deportation plans were themselves consciously genocidal. None of those seeking to drive out Jews to the Pripet marshes or to Siberia will have expected or hoped the deportees would thrive. As news spread among the Nazi elite of the events in the Soviet Union – and in the course of the summer we know that knowledge of what was happening to the Jews there became pretty widespread – so the sense of what it was to propose deportation to the Soviet Union must have changed too. When in August, for example, Nazi officials in France put forward the idea of deporting Europe's Jews to Russia, they were at the same time proposing not the separate existence of a Jewish people but its disappearance in hostile terrain. The miasma of killing was spreading out from the Soviet Union into the heads of key Nazis all across Europe.[16]

Death and deportation: September 1941

In March 1941 Hitler had resisted initiatives by Heydrich and Goebbels to dispatch Jews to Poland. In July 1941 he would reject attempts by Governor Frank to claim the Pripet marshes from the occupied Soviet territory and use them as a Jewish reservation. In August he blocked a new deportation plan from Heydrich. The war needed to be won before major deportations could be countenanced.

A variety of figures continued to urge not only deportations but also other special measures – above all decreeing that German Jews should wear a special star, something long established in Poland and now introduced in the Czech Protectorate. Goebbels, keen to make the pace and liberate Berlin of its sizeable Jewish presence, made a visit to Hitler on 18 August. Hitler did make some concessions. He agreed that German Jews should wear the Yellow Star – a considerable step and tacit recognition that voluntary emigration was no longer to be the anticipated fate of most German Jews. The star would make them easy to round up. Hitler promised too that Jews could be deported before the end of the war. But he still resisted any immediate action; the trains could be dispatched only after the eastern campaign was over.[17]

Some time in mid-September 1941, however, Hitler changed his mind. After meeting Otto Abetz, the German ambassador to France, who requested that all Jews be deported from occupied France, and hearing from the gauleiter of Hamburg, Karl Kaufmann, who wrote to Hitler requesting that Jewish housing be made available to German victims of the recent British bombing raids, Hitler now said that German Jews and those from the Czech Protectorate could be deported immediately.[18] Not only was the green light being given in relation to Germany's Jews, but other European Jews were also being readied for deportation. In the same month the deportation of French Jews, initially limited to those in detention, was also announced.[19]

In contrast to the onset of Operation Barbarossa, where we can see a clear stimulus to new actions, historians are less sure why Hitler should have decided now to reverse his previous line on deportations. The immediate trigger to act against Jews may have been the Soviets' sudden deportation of Volga Germans to Siberia on 13 to 15 September.[20] Hitler was a vengeful man and Goebbels's diary entry of 9 September (after Stalin's decision to deport the Volga Germans had been announced) makes clear the regime regarded Stalin's announcement as legitimation to take more radical steps.[21] For Hitler, it will have been a 'fitting' part of the revenge that the deportations of Jews began, in October, at exactly the point at which the Soviets were to have been defeated in the Nazis' original plans. He may have been helped to his decision by Rosenberg, the Minister for the Eastern Territories, who had concluded – no doubt on the basis of the Germans' own deportations – that most of the ethnic Germans would not survive the Soviet deportations. It was Rosenberg who on 14 September had passed on via his liaison officer at the Army High Command, Otto Bräutigam, the idea of deporting the Jews from central Europe to the east as a 'reprisal' to the Soviet action.[22]

At the very least, Hitler's decision on deportation was a significant radicalization of existing measures and a significant step closer to realizing his long-expressed desire to rid Europe of its Jews. But where were the Jews to go? Poland was no better equipped than it had been in August to take them. The Soviet campaign was not over. Hitler had given the green light for deportations under conditions no better than when he had previously blocked them. For some historians, this was crucial evidence that Hitler was now, in fact, either already decided on genocide, or on the brink of doing so.[23]

Other developments reinforce the idea that this was the decisive turning point. The policy of mass shootings began to cross the borders of the Soviet Union into Serbia and Galicia. Experiments in gassing Jews took place at Mogilev and in Minsk between 3 and 18 September. In the Warthegau the machinery of murder began to be put in place from October 1941. In November mobile gas vans were utilized there to murder Jews in the Kalisch district, while preparations at the Chelmno camp site date from the beginning of October. Within the Generalgouvernement, too, there were moves towards creating at least one gas camp. And sometime in the autumn the first experiments were carried out with cyanide at Auschwitz, though in the context of eliminating Soviet POWs.[24]

We will come back to these various initiatives in a moment, but we should note that Hitler's command for deportation did not tie in with them very neatly. Logically, if mass murder was already on the agenda, it would have made more sense to hold the Jews in Germany until the camps were ready.[25] Moreover, Hitler showed himself very uncertain over the following weeks as to whether the timing for deportations was opportune. This adds credence to the view that, in a rage at Soviet deportations of Volga Germans, Hitler had given in to a huge body of pressure without having formulated some new master plan. There is some evidence that Hitler was still restrained by the belief that until such point as the United States entered the war the Jews were useful as hostages. Four days after Hitler agreed to the deportations, Werner Koeppen, Rosenberg's personal aide, noted that the Führer had not yet made a decision about reprisals against German Jews. Koeppen had heard that Hitler would act if America entered the war.[26]

Thus when, as a temporary step, Hitler and Himmler agreed in September that 60,000 Jews should be deported not to the General-gouvernement but to the Łódź ghetto in the Wartheland, it seems deportation rather than murder was what they had in mind. As Himmler wrote to Arthur Greiser on 18 September, the plan was to deport Jews temporarily to the Łódź ghetto, and then on further east in spring 1942.[27] (In late September Hitler was again so confident about the military situation in the Soviet Union that this may have seemed a realistic timetable.)[28] After protests from Łódź, however, the figure was reduced to 25,000 Jews and gypsies. In early October, when Hitler added further to the numbers to be deported – calling for the entire Czech Protectorate to be cleared – he suggested that the Jews should not be sent to Poland but should immediately be directed further east, i.e. to the Soviet Union. It is obvious at the very least that the eventual extermination plan on Polish territory had not yet been arrived at, though it is unclear whether Hitler expected the deportees to be murdered on Soviet soil.[29]

The middle-managers of murder

Over the last decade or so our understanding of the events of these months has been transformed by a series of new regional studies, drawing on previously hidden German material held in Soviet Bloc archives. These studies have shown that while regional leaders may have responded to common signals and pressures, their various initiatives in these months were probably not part of a central plan.

From the summer of 1941 the notion spread that shooting Jews was an appropriate thing to do. Within the Soviet Union itself, we find in September and October all sorts of local units – including regular units of the German army – deciding off their own bat to extend the remit of their killing operations.[30] Outside the Soviet Union, in Serbia, the newly arrived commander, General Hans-Joachim Böhme, introduced a radical new reprisals policy against partisan attacks: all Jewish men of arms-bearing age were placed in a 'reservoir' of potential hostages and a hundred shot for every German soldier killed. Böhme made no distinction between different Jews or different patterns of behaviour. The official explanation given was that the Jews were linked to the partisan war. But it was clear that this was not the case. Even Jews who had been deported to Serbia from Austria, Bohemia and Danzig before the beginning of the partisan uprisings and had no conceivable relation to the partisan war were included in the murders. Böhme referred to these killings as shooting hostages. If these were 'hostages' this could only be in the abstract sense that the Germans were holding the abstract conspiratorial force 'World Jewry' to ransom.[31]

The killing ratio of a hundred to one was not Böhme's own idea but had been ordered from above. Moreover, soon after his arrival in Serbia in September he had been approached by German officials for a speedy resolution to the Jewish question. The officials, it seems, had been thinking of deportation. But though responding to such signals, Böhme had had no central instructions to make Jews his principal target. Instead, the historian Walter Manoschek has concluded that by the autumn of 1941 no special orders were necessary for such genocidal policy decisions to be taken. All the German authorities cooperated smoothly despite their disagreements in other questions. What is more, in this case the willingness to kill was not the result of the special indoctrination given to SS men. It was ordinary soldiers who carried out most of the murders. By the end of the year there was virtually no adult male Jewish population left in Serbia. Following the murder of the women and children in early 1942, Serbia became one of the first countries to be 'Jew free'.[32]

Eastern Galicia may well also offer a similar picture of regional initiative in response to the shooting lessons from the Soviet Union. On 12 October the security police embarked on a huge killing programme, eliminating thousands of men, women and children in the first two weeks, tens of thousands in the next couple of months.[33] Though Himmler held meetings with regional officials in early September and some post-war testimony intimated that a fundamental killing order was passed down the line, the report submitted in 1942 by the principal instigator of murders in the region, the Galician district SS and police leader (SSPF) Fritz Katzmann, does not support this. Himmler's direct orders are clearly confirmed only at much later points in the killing process – in July and October 1942 and May and October 1943. Of course, the fact that Himmler and above him Hitler were willing to endorse mass murder will have been known to all the officials in the area. But the shooting seems to have been a regional initiative designed in the short term to thin out the population so that 'manageable' ghettos could be created. Regional officials such as Katzmann were also certainly thinking of the possibility of total eradication of the Jews through murder.[34]

The killing lessons from the Soviet Union went further. Relatively early on Himmler drew the conclusion that some other form of murder might be preferable to shooting. The search for alternative methods probably began in July 1941 – there is a cryptic memo from Himmler about gas installations, and there is other evidence too that plans were already afoot then to gas Jews either on Soviet soil or in eastern Europe.[35] Other post-war testimony suggests that

Himmler was so badly affected by witnessing a shooting in August that he commissioned Arthur Nebe (or perhaps the HSSPF in central Russia, Erich von dem Bach-Zelewksi, who in turn commissioned Nebe) to develop alternatives, so as to avoid the spiritual burdening of his men. Nebe, as well as being the head of the Einsatzgruppe B, was also in charge of the institute involved in developing the mobile gas vans to kill mentally ill patients in Poland.

Perhaps in response to Himmler's concerns, perhaps independently, various local officials in the annexed Polish territories also began to wonder about other ways of getting rid of the Jews. Evidence of this is a notorious document stemming from the annexed Polish territories in the Warthegau. A memorandum sent to Eichmann on 16 July by the head of the SD in Posen, Rolf Heinz Höppner, summarized discussions under way among the advisers to the Reichsstaathalter, Greiser. A series of proposals had been made for dealing with the Jewish question. Those who could work should be in forced labour columns; women of childbearing age should be sterilized, so that with this generation the Jewish problem would be solved. In winter there would be the problem that not all the Jews could be fed. 'It should be seriously considered if the most humane solution would not be to kill those Jews not capable of work with some quick-acting means. This would certainly be more pleasant than allowing them to starve to death.' 'The things sound in part fantastical,' Höppner added, 'but in my view they are thoroughly practicable.'[36]

On 3 September Höppner sent another memorandum, thirteen pages long, proposing expanding the organization that existed in the annexed territories to handle deportations into the Generalgouvernement into a body that would handle deportations from a much wider source area – i.e. the whole Reich. He noted that fundamental decisions had not yet been made but asked about the final destination. He did not know the intentions of top officials. He imagined nevertheless that the Soviet territory would provide adequate space. But he said the important thing was to be sure of the Jews' final fate, and here he asked a question. 'Was the goal to guarantee them permanently the sure promise of life or was it to exterminate them completely'?[37]

This memorandum shows that there was still uncertainty, but also that the unthinkable was now being thought, at least in the Warthegau. What is not clear is how far Höppner was picking up signals from on high. Whatever the central input, Höppner was clearly responding to a growing sense both in the Warthegau (particularly in relation to Łódź) and in the Generalgouvernement that in the absence of immediate deportation the problems of food and epidemic raised by the Jewish population (i.e. by the Germans' treatment of them) required drastic action.

In the late summer and early autumn two new factors influenced policy in the annexed Polish provinces and in the Generalgouvernement. The first was Hitler's September decision to unleash the deportation trains. Whatever his immediate intentions, the eastward deportation of German Jews created new pressures and challenges for the receiving territories. Until then, the lack of capacity (above all in the Generalgouvernement) had repeatedly stymied the deportation aspirations of Heydrich and Eichmann. Now, the deportations were not to be blocked and the receiving authorities had to deal with the problem as far as they could. Despite the fiercest protests from the mayor of Łódź, from Kommissar Kube in Minsk, or from authorities in Latvia and Lithuania, the deportation trains started rolling.

Within two weeks of Himmler's edict that the first deportations should be sent to Łódź – an already overcrowded ghetto within the jurisdiction of the Wartheland authorities – construction began of the Chelmno gas camp. A letter sent by the Wartheland's Gauleiter Greiser to Himmler on 1 May 1942, looking back on events in 1941, indicates that the killing of 100,000 Polish Jews from the region was specifically authorized by Himmler, through Heydrich, as a quid pro quo for the willingness of the Wartheland authorities to receive deportees from Germany. While authorization for the killings came from the centre, the initiative had come from the locality, and the goal was the solution of a regional 'problem' rather than the implementation of a comprehensive programme.[38]

Unlike the annexed former Polish territory in the Wartheland, the Generalgouvernement proper was not directly affected by Hitler's deportations decision. Here, next to the 'shooting lessons' described above, the biggest impact of the Soviet campaign in the autumn was to disappoint earlier expectations of offloading the region's Jews. In the course of 1941 the whole of the administration, from Hans Frank downwards, had been anticipating the Jews' rapid removal into the territory of the former Soviet Union. But in mid-October Frank learned for sure that the slow progress of the war meant there was little prospect of such removals. The dragging Soviet campaign also had economic implications for his region. The failure to gain control of Soviet resources exacerbated German demands on foodstocks in the Generalgouvernement – and on top of everything else there was a very poor harvest in 1941. Pressure grew radically for the removal of 'useless mouths'.[39] For Frank's staff the Jews represented a constant source of illegal activity; not surprising given that the restrictions imposed on Polish Jews denied them any legal opportunity to earn enough even just to survive. A fatal two-pronged development ensued. The hardline radicals in Himmler's almost autonomous police empire in Poland undertook violent initiatives, while the civilian administration imposed ordinances of exclusion and persecution on the Jewish population, which made killing seem the only option.[40]

The Lublin district SSPF, Odilo Globocnik, had shown ruthless energy in developing murderous labour projects for Jews in the Bug region. In 1941 he unfolded far-reaching plans to Germanize Lublin, expelling all Poles and Jews from the area. On 20 July 1941 Himmler gave him a special commission to prepare the ground for German settlement of the Lublin district and then further east. At the beginning of October Globocnik urgently sought a meeting with Himmler to discuss radical proposals for clearing the Lublin area of its Jews. Globocnik's letter of 1 October suggests that up till then he had heard nothing of a comprehensive programme of murder. His meeting with Himmler took place on 13 October, the same day that Governor Frank discovered for sure that no deportations were likely to take place in the near future. The outcome of Globocnik's consultations was the decision to begin building an extermination camp at Bełżec. At a meeting on 17 October, Globocnik, Frank and others met to agree that the Lublin area should be cleared of Jews. Although they talked about 'Jews being transferred across the Bug river', it is clear – since all participants knew by then that such deportations were impossible – that this was a euphemism for murder.[41]

What is hotly disputed is exactly what the camp's remit was. The initially rather limited scale of the building programme may suggest that this was more of an experimental camp than part of a comprehensive murder programme. Bełżec consisted of a few wooden buildings, staffed until the arrival of former euthanasia personnel in November by only three SS people. On the other hand, quite small camps would prove able to murder an extraordinarily large number of people, so the camp's size is not immediately proof of the modest ambitions. At the very least, the murder of the hundreds of thousands of Lublin Jews was being contemplated. But there is some evidence that the authorities in the Generalgouvernement as a whole were now assuming that the Jewish population there would soon all be eliminated. In other words, even if the creation of the Bełżec camp responded to Globocnik's initiative in Lublin, it seems possible that expectations within the Generalgouvernement as a whole rapidly emerged of the murder of Polish Jews.[42]

The crystallization of genocide

The thrust of this recent research, then, is to suggest that the slippage from murderously neglectful and brutal occupation policies to genocidal measures took place initially without a comprehensive set of commands from the centre. The centre, above all Himmler, was consulted in almost all the cases we have looked at. But neither Hitler nor Himmler was providing a clear-cut plan or even a fundamental command for the lower echelons to carry out.

What then was the role of Hitler, Himmler and Heydrich in these

months? Let us be clear that, without Hitler, none of the developments would have happened. It was he who brought the agenda of
anti-Semitism to centre stage and, just as important, he who imposed
the fundamental tenor of warfare and occupation. The failure of
humanitarian impulses to exercise any restraint on regime activity
was down to him. Perhaps the last check had fallen when Hitler had
expressly overruled the army's humanitarian concerns in the Polish
campaign.[43] Every action taken against Jews by lower level officials
was legitimated by the shared knowledge of Hitler's own radical
anti-Semitic agenda. His public pronouncements against Jews were
legion.[44] For example, he repeatedly returned to his 'prophecy'.[45]
Whatever Hitler's precise intentions, his rhetoric thus provided the
legitimation for others' actions, giving the perpetrators assurance
that murder was appropriate.

Though the evidence is less clear here, the regime was so focused
on Hitler that it seems likely that fundamental new moves on the
Jewish question had his imprimatur. As evidence of the need to
consult Hitler on killings consider the fact that when Wilhelm Koppe
in the Warthegau asked Himmler if 30,000 Poles suffering from
tuberculosis could be killed, the answer was that the Führer's
approval was required.[46] Even where Hitler concealed his involvement, therefore, we know that responsibility was his. The question
this leaves open in relation to Jewish affairs, as the Serbian case
shows, is what did Hitler's subordinates believe was already covered
by their existing remit and what required new authorization? Many
historians have seen it as probable that in October 1941 Hitler gave
approval for the killings of Wartheland Jews at Chelmno and for
killing Jews in Bełżec. There is no evidence of his involvement; but
the general functioning of the system makes it likely.

Whatever meaning Hitler attached to the deportation decision in
September, Heydrich's approach to the deportations bordered on the
genocidal from the start. The preparations of the security police in
Łódź suggest that Heydrich was assuming from the beginning that a
large part of the deportees would die, though not necessarily be shot
outright. The Gestapo in Łódź were planning to divide the ghetto

into two; one section for working Jews and a much smaller one for the larger number of non-working Jews. The clear implication was that the latter were to die of hunger and disease. In October, once it was clear that Łódź would receive only a small share of the envisaged deportees, Heydrich looked to the Baltic and Byelorussia. At a meeting on the 10th Heydrich's approach to the deportations of Czech Jews in particular was even more radical.[47] He explicitly stated that the Jews to be deported to Riga and Minsk should be the most burdensome (*lästigste*), i.e. least capable of working. Some authors have assumed he was envisaging that they would be shot by the Einsatzgruppen;[48] more recently, Christian Gerlach has raised the possibility that preparations for an extermination camp at Mogilev may have some connection with these deportations.[49] Whatever the precise conception, Heydrich seems to have been thinking of very low survival rates: for those Czech Jews not on the first deportation lists, he planned to create separate ghettos for those able to work and those dependent on relief (*Versorgungslager*), and envisaged that the Jewish communities would be decimated before they were even shoved on to the trains.[50]

In other words, even though there was not yet a precise concept of killing the deportees by gas, the dividing line between the territorial solution and that of outright murder was becoming very thin indeed. On 23 October all Jewish emigration from the Reich was prohibited. On the 25th Erhard Wetzel, the official in charge of race questions in Rosenberg's Ministry of the East wrote to the Reich commissioner for the Ostland, Hinrich Lohse, recommending the deployment of the former euthanasia personnel to construct gas installations in order to eliminate deported Jews who were unfit to work.[51] The 'territorial' element of sending the Jews east was becoming more and more of a metaphor. Selection and attrition were becoming the central elements of the process, rather than desirable by-products.

In mid-November Himmler and Rosenberg had a lengthy meeting after which Rosenberg provided a detailed press briefing. Here the distance between deportation and destruction had narrowed to nothing. Though the issue of killing – as against allowing to die – was not yet spelled out and Rosenberg still used the metaphor of deportation, his reference to the 'biological eradication of the entire Jewry of Europe' made absolutely explicit that extinction and not just removal of Jewish presence was the aim.[52] At almost exactly the same time, on 16 November, Goebbels published in the journal *Das Reich* a leading article that was excerpted in many of the German regional papers.[53] Entitled 'The Jews are guilty', the piece provided one of the most explicit communications to the German people as a whole that Jews were going to be exterminated. World Jewry, Goebbels wrote, was suffering a gradual annihilation process. Jews were falling according to their own law – an eye for an eye, a tooth for a tooth. In December Goebbels acknowledged in his diary that the deportation of Jews to the east was 'in many cases synonymous with the death penalty'.[54]

On 25 October 1941 Himmler and Heydrich were having dinner with Hitler at the Führer's headquarters. Hitler referred to his prophecy and went on:

Let no one say to me, we cannot send them into the swamp! Who takes any interest in *our* people? It is good if our advance is preceded by fear that we will exterminate Jewry. The attempt to create a Jewish state will end in failure.[55]

There is a hint here that Hitler was now rejecting any kind of territorial solution. His reference to swamp (*Morast*), suggests an acknowledgement that he knew of the efforts by the SS to drown Jewish women and children in the Pripet marshes.[56] But at other times he still spoke as though deportation to a reservation remained the policy.

The historian Shlomo Aronson has argued that around this time Hitler lost interest in Jews as hostages. Roosevelt's declaration on 11 September that the US navy would shoot on sight Axis warships in waters essential for American defence was one turning point.[57] It is possible that his decision to extend Lend Lease to Moscow on 1 October was the final straw.[58] On 28 November Hitler met the Grand Mufti of Jerusalem. Hitler was seeking to court him – aware, no doubt, that just a few years earlier the Nazis had been working together with Jewish agencies to 'facilitate' Jewish emigration to Palestine. Some of what he said will have been for effect. But still, Hitler's declaration, which he requested the Grand Mufti to 'lock deep into his heart', was striking.[59] For the sake of pleasing him, Hitler needed to have specified only that the Germans would deport the Jews to Siberia, along the lines of his statement to Kvaternik in the summer.[60] But he went much further. After a successful war, Hitler said, Germany would have only one remaining objective in the Middle East: the annihilation of the Jews living under British protection in Arab lands. There was not a shadow of a territorial solution left.

Another indication of the hardening of attitudes was the evolving treatment of the German-Jewish deportees. Up to 8 November 20,000 German, Austrian and Czech Jews and 5,000 gypsies had been deported to Łódź. Because of the successful protests of the Łódź authorities, during the following three months over 30,000 more were deported to Minsk, Kovno and Riga. What happened to these Jews was extremely variable. Those sent to Łódź were interned in the ghetto. The Jews dispatched to Minsk were similarly housed in ghettos – in this case made vacant by the murders of the previous occupants. Though living conditions were horrendous, indeed barely survivable, the deportees were not murdered. Transport shortages meant that only seven of the eighteen Minsk transports planned for 1941 actually took place; the last was dispatched on 19 November. The proposed camp in Riga was not yet ready, so in the following week five transports were sent instead to Kovno in Lithuania. All the occupants were murdered on arrival in the infamous Fort IX. The first deportees to Riga, arriving there on 30 November, were also massacred. Up to early December 1941 then, 'only' six out of the forty-one transports of Reich Jews had been murdered on arrival; all the murders had taken place at the end of November.[61]

There is considerable debate surrounding the reason for these latter murders, particularly the killing of Berlin Jews in Riga. On 29 and 30 November, just before the deportees' arrival, 4,000 Latvian Jews in the Riga ghettos had been murdered under the auspices of the HSSPF in the Baltic, Friedrich Jeckeln, and the local head of the security police (KdS), Rudolf Lange. On 30 November Himmler telephoned Heydrich from the Führer's headquarters with the message 'Jewish transports from Berlin. No liquidation.'[62] The message was duly sent on to Riga – too late: the Berlin deportees had been included in the shooting. The historian Richard Breitman discovered in the Public Records Office the British intercept of an angry message from Himmler to his HSSPF: 'The Jews resettled into the territory of the Ostland are to be dealt with only according to the guidelines given by me and the Reich Security Main Office acting on my behalf. I will punish unilateral acts and violations.'[63] Such a message seems hard to reconcile with a pre-established plan to murder all German Jews. But then the lack of reaction to the murders in Kovno confirms the sense gained from Heydrich's guidelines that there was no particular concern about killing German Jews either. Instead, murder was at the very least being tolerated, indeed there is a sense that 'policy-drift' was deliberately being cultivated from above without a comprehensive decision having been made.

So why in this case the angry telegram? Breitman believes it arose from a specific issue – the inclusion in the transport of Jewish Iron Cross holders who should have been sent to Theresienstadt.[64] But the urgency with which Jeckeln was summoned to Berlin for talks thereafter suggests more was at stake. We know that Hitler and Himmler were intensely sensitive to issues of morale and public opinion. Or, as Goebbels put it just eight days earlier, the Führer 'wants an energetic policy against the Jews, which, however, does not cause us unnecessary difficulties'.[65] The transports of German Jews to Minsk and the Baltic and the inclusion of German Jews in the killing process had led to a large number of questions and concerns being raised by different groups. Some officials, notably Generalkommissar Kube, in Minsk, had expressed reluctance to kill German Jews. Even though such qualms were demonstrably ineffective in stopping deportations, they were probably beginning to raise some concerns in Berlin. We know from Bernhard Lösener, the expert on Jewish matters in the Ministry of the Interior, that rumours about the murders of the Berlin Jews at Riga were doing the rounds there.[66] Probably Himmler and perhaps Hitler decided final consultations were needed before more German Jews could be eliminated.

The argument here then is that the dissemination and modification of the Soviet experiment took place piecemeal, by improvisation and example, over the period from September to November 1941. Himmler and Heydrich were closely involved; Hitler's involvement is less well documented, though he would at the very least have known what was happening, and at the very least would have decided not to prevent it. To stay on this course Himmler would have needed Hitler's approving nod, though how emphatic that was, we do not know. In the course of October and November Hitler, Himmler and those around them made statements showing how rapidly the idea of a territorial solution was dissolving into a mere metaphor. The territories were becoming holding bays before death. Whatever Hitler's green light for deportations had meant in September, by the end of November the idea of a reservation had effectively disappeared. In late November, as we will see, Himmler held a concerted series of consultations on the Jewish issue. It seems that as the overall concept of genocide crystallized in the heads of Nazi leaders, so other agencies had to be brought on board.

There is no smoking-gun evidence for this chronology or the relationship between killing decisions and killing actions that lies behind it. We cannot definitively rule out the possibility that Hitler had already decided on genocide much earlier in the summer of 1941. Conversely, for some historians, it was only later – in December 1941, or even in spring or early summer 1942 – that the final moment of decision took place. It is time now to test our approach against the evidence of the Wannsee conference itself.

4

The villa, the lake, the meeting

Invitations to a conference

In November 1941 Reinhard Heydrich was at the height of his career. Born in Halle of musical parents and a gifted violinist himself, he had grown up in the turbulent conditions of the 1920s. Political upheavals and economic crises after the First World War hit his family hard and university study was out of the question. Having admired the navy as a child, Heydrich sought a career as a naval officer. But in 1931 that plan ended in disaster when his treatment of a former fiancée was (rather unfairly) deemed conduct unbecoming to an officer. Recruited by Himmler to run his fledgling intelligence service, the SD, Heydrich rose rapidly behind his master. A driven and demanding man, he was something of a charismatic figure. An enthusiastic fencer, he was also a trained pilot, and quixotically took time off from his job to fly a Messerschmitt ME109 in the attack on Norway in April 1940. In September 1941 Heydrich finally came out of Himmler's shadow, when Hitler appointed him deputy (and de facto acting) Protector for the occupied Czech territories. In typical Nazi style, Heydrich did not give up his existing office but merely added the posts together, commuting regularly between Prague and Berlin. With a mixture of ruthlessness and a degree of flexibility, Heydrich soon made his mark in the Czech Protectorate. At the time of the Wannsee conference, Heydrich was thus head of the Reichssicherheitshauptamt (the body combining the Gestapo, the criminal police and the SD for the whole of Germany), Reich

Protector in the occupied Czech territory and one of the most feared and powerful men in Germany. He was thirty-seven.[1]

Heydrich's assistant, who would do much of the donkey-work for the Wannsee conference, was a far less colourful character. Indeed, it was Adolf Eichmann's lack of stature or demonic quality at Jerusalem that led Hannah Arendt to coin the concept of the 'banality of evil'. Born in Solingen and of modest background, during the 1920s Eichmann did his apprenticeship as a salesman, afterwards working for an oil company in Linz. In 1933 he moved back to Germany and trained in the armed SS until the SD offered him the chance to explore his bureaucratic talents, at first as a relatively lowly official. His breakthrough came in 1938 with the establishment of the office to promote Jewish emigration in Vienna. Here Eichmann showed the energy, ruthlessness and ability to extract compliance from the Jewish officials under him that was to be his hallmark. When the RSHA was created, Eichmann became head of its Jewish section, and was one of the principal organizers of the attempted transports of German Jews. At the time of the conference he was thirty-five.

Towards the end of November 1941 Heydrich had Eichmann draft some rather wordy invitations:

On the 31 July 1941 the Reich Marshal of the Greater German Reich commissioned me, with the assistance of the other central authorities, to make all necessary organisational and technical preparations for a comprehensive solution of the Jewish Question and to present him with a comprehensive proposal at an early opportunity. A photocopy of his instructions is attached to this letter.

Given the extraordinary significance pertaining to these questions and in the interest of achieving a common view among the central agencies involved in the relevant tasks, I propose to hold a meeting on these issues. This is all the more important because since the 15th October 1941 transports of Jews from the Reich territory, including the Protectorate of Bohemia and Moravia, have been regularly evacuated to the East. I therefore invite you to a meeting . . .[2]

The invitations went out between 29 November and 1 December. The meeting, followed by a buffet, was to be held on 9 December at an address given as the 'offices of Interpol, 16 Am Kleinen Wannsee'.[3] A subsequent memo of 4 December altered the venue to an SS guesthouse, 56–58 Am Großen Wannsee.[4] What needed to be clarified on the Jewish question? What kind of preparations needed still to be made? We do not have much evidence of Heydrich's thinking in these days, but we do have the names he put on his guest list.[5] Whom had he invited and why were they there?

Heydrich's guests were important men, for the most part of equivalent status (though none with equivalent power) to himself. Most were Staatssekretäre, Unterstaatssekretäre or the Party equivalents thereof, ranks equivalent to under-secretary of state in the US or permanent secretary in the British civil service or their respective deputies.[6] 'Those were the gentlemen', as prosecutor Robert Kempner reminded one of the many truculent Wannsee participants after the war, claiming to have known nothing about anything, 'who knew the things you had to know'.[7] Kempner had good reason to be confident of his judgement – in the Weimar era he had been a rising civil servant himself before fleeing to the United States. After 1933 the Staatssekretäre if anything increased in importance. With cabinet government disabled in the Third Reich and Hitler practically forbidding his ministers from meeting independently, it was the fifty or so Staatssekretäre who were the essential medium of policy coordination. When new organizations like the Four-Year Plan emerged, for example, they 'borrowed' Staatssekretäre from the relevant ministries to act as the coordinating organizations. Meetings between the Staatssekretäre were in effect a substitute for cabinet government.

Heydrich's first list of names comprised two main groups. The largest one consisted of the representatives of ministries with responsibilities for the Jewish question, including representatives from the Ministries of the Interior, Justice, Economics and Propaganda, the Reich Chancellery, the Foreign Ministry and the Ministry for the Occupied Eastern Territories. The other guests were all from Party and SS agencies with special interest in race questions. Heydrich invited men from the Party Chancellery, the SS Main Office for Race and Settlement and the Office of the Reich Kommissar for the Strengthening of Germandom.

Looking at these candidates, we can rule out from the beginning the idea sometimes still voiced that Heydrich was planning to talk about the technical details of transports.[8] The problem of finding locations for transports was undoubtedly pressing. Łódź's intake had been sharply reduced, Minsk had been shut down for a while and Riga's absorptive capacity was limited. But quite apart from the fact that the Staatssekretäre were too senior to be called together for such matters, Heydrich had not invited any transport specialist, or a military representative or indeed anyone from the Finance Ministry. Deportation arrangements were not to be on the agenda.

Very many of those on Heydrich's original list were in one way or other involved in determining the status of Jews and dealing with the cases of 'Mischlinge' (the Nazi-invented category of mixed-race Jews) and mixed marriages. Indeed, for some of his proposed guests – the Party Chancellery representative and the Justice Ministry's man – such status questions were the principal point of their involvement with the Jewish question. The guest list lends itself to the interpretation, therefore, that the Mischlinge and the borderline cases were to be high on the agenda.[9]

The historian Christian Gerlach has argued recently that the guest list was initially restricted to parties interested specifically in German Jews and only later gained a European dimension. Gerlach argues that this shift adds credence to his view that Hitler committed himself to genocide on a European scale only in December 1941. It is certainly the case that the representative for occupied Poland was added as an afterthought.[10] On 28 November, before the invitations went out but after the provisional list had been drawn up, Heydrich and Himmler were visited by the police and SS chief in the Generalgouvernement, HSSPF Krüger, the latter bemoaning his difficulties with Governor Frank. Only now did Heydrich decide to invite to his meeting civilian and security police representatives from Poland.[11]

It is indeed interesting that these representatives had not been on his initial list. Whatever else Heydrich first had in mind, it was clearly not a detailed discussion of the murder arrangements that were soon to fall into place in the Generalgouvernement. Yet we should not read too much into the change. It took place very soon after the original guest list was drawn up. No one else with responsibility outside the Reich was added later (though some of Heydrich's own staff at the meeting did have responsibilities outside Germany, and it is possible they were brought in only in December).[12] The list in any case included delegates with international interests – two from the Ministry for the Occupied Eastern Territories as well as one from the Foreign Office. What the Krüger affair indicates rather more strongly is that Heydrich was particularly concerned to include departments with whom he and Himmler had experienced difficulty. Resolving demarcation disputes and streamlining responsibilities were near the top of his agenda.

Many of those invited were unsure what Heydrich wanted. For some, any kind of summons from the RSHA was a matter of dread. Since there was no agenda beyond the wording of the invitation itself, all sorts of interpretations were possible. The Ministry of the Interior had had the instructive experience not long before of sending a delegate to a meeting organized by Eichmann, only to find the agenda far broader than the one ostensibly tabled.[13] Still, on this occasion the ministry thought it knew what was pending. One of its representatives, Dr Feldscher, informed a counterpart in the Ministry for the Eastern Territories that the Wannsee conference had been called to achieve a 'breakthrough' on the treatment of mixed-race Jews. A few days later the Interior Ministry's expert on Jewish questions drew up a defensive paper, anticipating a new challenge to existing guidelines.[14] Dr Feldscher, however, evidently believed that the meeting would discuss proposals for a settlement of the Jewish question to be effected only *after* the war, showing that he was far from up to speed on current proposals. For his part, Martin Luther, who ran the German department for the Foreign Ministry, believed the conference had a quite different scope, as a 'wish-list' drawn up on 8 December makes clear.[15] The Foreign Ministry clearly expected to be discussing the collection and deportation of Jews in countries all across Europe.[16]

Postponing the meeting

The Staatssekretäre had rather longer to guess what awaited them than they might have expected. On 8 December Heydrich's staff telephoned round, deferring the meeting indefinitely.[17] The news of the Japanese attack on Pearl Harbor had reached Germany the evening before and it seems almost certain that it was this that put the gathering on hold. For one thing, the policy implications would need to be considered. For another, a number of the participants, including Heydrich himself, were members of the Reichstag and were likely to have to attend. After Japan had opened hostilities in the Pacific, it was known that Hitler wanted to follow suit and enjoy the psychological advantage of declaring war on the USA before Roosevelt had a chance to make his own declaration. This would involve calling a special Reichstag session.[18] The other factor delaying the conference would have been the sudden dramatic worsening of conditions on the Eastern Front in early December. For a while, the future of any eastern policy was in doubt.

Christian Gerlach argues that it was only now in early December that Hitler finally decided to murder all European Jews. On 12 December at a meeting of Reich and Gau leaders of the Nazi Party, Hitler made some very strong statements (if Goebbels's diary is an accurate record):

As regards the Jewish Question, the Führer has decided to sweep the floor clean. He had prophesied to the Jews that if they ever caused a world war again, they would suffer extermination. This was not just mere phrasemaking. The world war is upon us; the extermination of the Jews is the necessary consequence. This question should be regarded without any sentimentality. We are not here to sympathise with the Jews but to sympathise with our German people. With the German people having once more sacrificed

160,000 dead in the campaign in the East, then the original agents of this bloody conflict must pay for it with their lives.[19]

This was a pithy and hard-edged instance of Hitler's prophecy. It followed one day after his Reichstag declaration of war against the United States. Four days later one of the participants, Hans Frank, gave a speech at a government meeting in the Generalgouvernement, in which he said he was pushing for the Jews to go east. A large Jewish migration would begin, he said:

But what shall we do with the Jews? Do you think they are going to be settled in new villages in the West? They said to us in Berlin: why cause us all this bother, we too have no use for them in the Baltic or in the Reich Commissariat, liquidate them yourselves! . . .[20]

These 3.5 million Jews – we can't shoot them, we can't poison them, but we will have to take steps to destroy them somehow, above all in connection with the measures to be discussed in the Reich.[21]

Seldom had any German official indicated more clearly that transport to the east meant murder.

Alongside these echoes of Hitler's message to the faithful, a second piece of evidence that some decisive change had taken place is a memorandum dated 16 December from Rosenberg, the Reich Minister for Eastern Territories, concerning a meeting with Hitler two days before. Rosenberg had drafted a major foreign policy speech and Hitler had evidently responded that Japan's entry into the war had changed the situation. Rosenberg noted:

On the Jewish question I said that now, after the decision, the references to the New York Jews should perhaps be altered. I took the view that we should not talk about the destruction [*Ausrottung*] of the Jews. The Führer agreed and said that they had imposed the war on us, they had brought destruction, so it should be no wonder if the consequences hit them first.[22]

Finally, there is an entry in Himmler's appointments calendar following a meeting with Hitler on 18 December, '*Judenfrage.* | *als Partisanen auszurotten*' ('Jewish question | to be eliminated as partisans').

Gerlach believes this can be taken as a generic commitment to murdering Jews, particularly when taken in the context of other meetings and remarks around the same time.

As so often given the fluctuating character of Hitler's pronouncements, the fragments in themselves cannot be conclusive. When compared with his comments to Goebbels in August 1941 and to Himmler and Heydrich in October or his subsequent remarks in 1942, December seems less obviously *the* moment of clarity. Hitler gave his speech just a day after the decision to wage war on the USA. At such moments he was at his most vehement; just as in the wake of the news about the Volga Germans' fate he had unleashed the deportations of German Jews. In January, however, Hitler's table talk reverted to the ambiguity. On 25 January 1942, for example, 'the Jew must leave Europe' – though with a warning that if the Jew chose not to emigrate, then there would be extermination (and this after emigration had been banned!).[23] On 27 January he was once again using the – metaphor? – of deportation, 'The Jew must leave Europe! The best thing would be for them to go to Russia.' A few days later he was more obscure again – the Jew had to 'disappear' from Europe.[24] Viewed over time there is perhaps a discernible displacement from autumn 1941 onwards; but the thinking is too erratic and fluctuates too much to provide clear cut-offs or singular turning points. On the other hand, we know that even in his small circle of close advisers Hitler would sometimes pretend his views or knowledge were different from what they were. There is no proof, therefore, that when he talked of deportations he really deluded himself into thinking Jews were not being killed.[25]

Our own uncertainty about Hitler's thoughts, however, would not matter if we could show his *subordinates* were sure they had heard the decisive word. The Himmler jotting about partisans seems far too fragmentary to be considered proof of anything, particularly as supporting arguments involving meetings with Philippe Bouhler and Viktor Brack are themselves circumstantial. Rosenberg's memo lends itself to a slightly different interpretation. Rosenberg himself claimed at the Nuremberg Trials that the 'decision' to which he had referred was that of entering the war against the USA, and in the German text this does seem the more plausible reading.[26] The rather abstract concept 'The Decision', without qualification, makes sense if it follows on from the talk about war, particularly as it belonged to the language of fate and destiny with which the Nazis referred to war. And in Nazi thinking, it might be argued there was a logic here: before, open threats might have deterred the 'Jewish' enemy from taking on Germany; now, the threats had no purchase. In short, Rosenberg's comments might just as well be taken to mean that a pre-existing policy of extermination should be dealt with differently in public rhetoric, now that the war with the USA had begun.[27] The episode does confirm, however, how much further down the road to genocide Hitler had travelled since his deportation decision of September. Though he had probably long given up on influencing Roosevelt, the declaration of war closed the chapter (some dismal wartime negotiations notwithstanding) of using the Jews as diplomatic hostages. Until now, Hitler's strongest remarks had tended to be made to his absolutely closest aides, but here he was making the gesture of informing some fifty of his top lieutenants of his plans. This was a major event. Such a statement could only help clarify the authority with which Himmler and Heydrich pushed forward their murderous vision. Party figures now had a stronger sense than ever of the leadership's commitment to murder.

On 8 January Heydrich sent a note to those invited to Wannsee expressing regret at the previous postponement. The explanation offered was hardly enlightening: 'events which had suddenly intruded and the resulting commitments of some of the invited participants'. Heydrich now suggested meeting on 20 January.[28] The conference had thus been deferred for almost six weeks. Did this indicate, as Eberhard Jäckel has suggested, that the event was relatively unimportant? Heydrich's note talked rather of the urgency of the issues involved. Probably the lengthy delay was a reflection of the protracted period of uncertainty on the Eastern Front and the lack of any spare transport capacity at the time (though the latter problem would continue to March). By 8 January, though the situation was still extremely critical, the Germans could at least hope they would suc-ceed in stabilizing the military situation.[29] Plans for deportation and murder could go ahead.

A villa in Wannsee

Wannsee is a beautiful suburb to the south-west of Berlin. Largely undeveloped until the mid nineteenth century, the area took off when the banker Wilhelm Conrad decided to build luxurious dwellings for wealthy refugees from the summer heat of the capital. In the latter decades of the nineteenth century the area's rich villas and exotic gardens became the preferred summer residences of the Berlin upper middle class. From October to Easter Wannsee slumbered peacefully, but in the summer months it filled up with top board members from the big banks and industry, scientists and artists. Ironically, given its later connotations, the name of Wannsee was then associated with cosmopolitanism and a good measure of tolerance. Christians and acculturated or converted German Jews lived reasonably comfort-ably side by side. Their afterlife was similarly harmonious, since both faiths were buried in the same cemetery, the Neue Friedhof, whose walls bear both a cross and a star of David. The architect responsible for the Wannsee conference villa also designed the house of one of Weimar's most progressive spirits, the artist Max Liebermann. Living just a stone's throw away from what would become one of the most notorious addresses in the world, Liebermann, a leading impression-ist and President of the Prussian Academy of Arts, epitomized the 'other', tolerant and liberal-minded Germany.[30]

After 1933 Wannsee's beauty and tranquillity attracted a string of leading Nazis. Josef Goebbels, Walther Funk, Hermann Esser, Wilhelm Stuckart – one of those invited by Heydrich – Hitler's doctor, Dr Morell, and many other Nazi luminaries acquired proper-ties there. Like many of them, Albert Speer obtained his villa on the cheap at the expense of former Jewish owners. A number of Nazi organizations and foundations bought up properties too. The Nazi

Women's League established its Reich Bride School here; the National Socialist Welfare NSV placed a training school in one of the villas. The SS set up several institutes in the area and the SD had been holding conferences there since 1936.

The villa at 56–58 Am Großen Wannsee enjoyed a marvellous view over the larger of the two Wannsee lakes, on whose western shore it lay. It had belonged to Friedrich Minoux, a right-wing industrialist with the Stinnes concern.[31] In 1940, under investigation for fraud, Minoux sold the villa to an SD charitable foundation, the Stiftung Nordhav. Ostensibly the foundation's purpose was to construct holiday and convalescent homes for SD members, though it seems possible that its aim also was to acquire properties on Heydrich's behalf. After Minoux handed the house over in May 1941, the residence was converted into a guesthouse for senior security police and SD personnel visiting Berlin.[32]

In selecting the villa as the venue for the meeting, Heydrich had thus eschewed more intimidating or business-like locations. Instead he had gone for expansiveness and informality. The guesthouse's publicity leaflet promised

completely refurbished guest rooms, a music room and games room (billiards), a large meeting room and conservatory, a terrace looking on to the Wannsee, central heating, hot and cold running water and all comforts. The house offers good food, including lunch and dinner. Wine, beer and cigarettes are available.

For all of which the cost was a very reasonable 5RM per night including service and breakfast.[33]

Heydrich's guests

On a snowy Tuesday morning, 20 January 1942, some fifteen senior officials gathered at the SD villa by the Wannsee lake.[34] Not everyone on Heydrich's original invitation list had come. The Propaganda Ministry's representative must have been otherwise engaged, since although he did not attend on this occasion the minister expressed a burning interest in attending follow-up meetings.[35] Ulrich Greifelt, the Director of the Staff Office for the Reich Commissar for the Strengthening of Germandom, also failed to show; he may have been on other business in Italy. The guests originally proposed from the Generalgouvernement had been replaced by their subordinates. On the civilian side, it was Hans Frank's deputy, Josef Bühler, who attended, while the head of the security policy for the Generalgouvernement (BdS), Eberhard Schöngarth, came as security police representative for the area.[36] For the Justice Ministry, Franz Schlegelberger, though Staatssekretär in rank, was at this time acting minister, and he sent a deputy, Roland Freisler, the later infamous president of the People's Court.

The largest group round the table comprised the representatives of ministries with responsibilities for the Jewish question – thus Wilhelm Stuckart (Interior), Roland Freisler (Justice), Erich Neumann (Four-Year Plan organization), Friedrich-Wilhelm Kritzinger (Reich Chancellery), Martin Luther (Foreign Ministry). The two representatives of the Ministry for the Eastern Territories, Alfred Meyer and Georg Leibbrandt, fell into this category, but, together with Josef Bühler from the Generalgouvernement, they formed a second group, namely German agencies with responsibilities for civilian administration of occupied territories in the east. Then there were the officials from the SS and Party with special interest in race questions – Gerhard Klopfer (Party Chancellery) and Otto Hofmann (SS Main Office for Race and Settlement). In addition Heydrich had also instructed officials from his own security empire to attend. The most senior was Heydrich's direct subordinate, the Gestapo-head and chief of RSHA Department IV, Heinrich Müller, and below him, Adolf Eichmann. From the field there were Eberhard Schöngarth, the BdS in the Generalgouvernement, and Rudolf Lange, the head of Einsatzkommando 2 and regional chief of the security police in Riga. It is just possible that Eichmann's deputy, Rolf Günther, was present to take notes.

These were influential and for the most part well-educated men.

Two thirds had a university degree, and over half bore the title of doctor, mainly in law. At the same time, they were strikingly young. Almost half were under forty, only two fifty or over. Youth was particularly apparent among the Party, SS and security police representatives, five of whom were in their thirties. On the civilian side also, ambitious young men were at the table. Wilhelm Stuckart, the second most important man in the Ministry of the Interior (in view of the ineffectiveness of Minister Frick, perhaps *the* most important man) was only thirty-nine.

With what expectations and feelings did the assembled gentlemen enter Minoux's former villa that day? There will be much to say in a moment about how it was that these men assented to genocide, but as to their mood on that morning we can only speculate. Those who survived the war and were brought to trial in the immediate post-war years denied having attended at all. After the Protocol was found they affected only pale reminiscences. Adolf Eichmann spoke more openly, but particularly on his aspirations his testimony is unreliable, concerned as he was to portray himself as mere dutiful errand boy, with neither initiative nor knowledge. So we can only guess what they felt. And yet, we can be fairly certain that they did not all come with the same spirit or expectations. Heydrich's men and his guests from the SS and the Party hoped that the meeting would further radicalize the Jewish agenda and wrest power from the ministries. The ministries were by and large on the defensive, seeking to protect their waning influence from further incursions of the security police. Of all the participants, Wilhelm Stuckart had most cause to feel beleaguered. He would have suspected, quite rightly, that the meeting's function was to subordinate the civilian agencies, and above all his own ministry, to the insistent claims of Heydrich's RSHA.

The Protocol of the young men of Berlin

Before the meeting convened, Eichmann tells us, the assembled worthies stood around in groups and chatted for a while; then they got down to business. The formal proceedings were relatively short – perhaps an hour to an hour and a half. With no agenda, much of the time was taken up by an extensive lecture from Heydrich. It seems there were some interjections from the other participants and a little more other discussion afterwards. But these are conjectures. We have no direct transcript of what was said. A stenotypist took the minutes in shorthand (it is probably Eichmann's invention that there was a second SS official, his deputy, Rolf Günther, also taking notes)[37] but the minutes have not been preserved. In any case they were not verbatim, according to Eichmann, and recorded only the salient points.[38] What we have is the Protocol, or in other words Eichmann's glossary of the notes, which he claimed was in turn heavily edited by Heydrich.

The Protocol is thus very far from a verbatim account. 'These weren't records,' Heinrich Lammers, the head of the Reich Chancellery, protested at Nuremberg. 'They're just one-sided minutes, compiled in the RSHA.'[39] For many of our questions, that does not really matter. The Protocol reflects the purposes and interests of the man who called the meeting – Reinhard Heydrich – and is in many ways as important as anything he said on the day. Perhaps more so, since the Protocol reflects what he wanted written down and recorded. When the participants received it, they learned what it was he wanted them to know, whether or not it accorded with their own memory of what had been discussed at the meeting itself. For this reason, some of the civil servants' post-war denials that murder had been discussed at the meeting are beside the point. Perhaps not surprisingly, no one dared submit criticisms or amendments to Heydrich, though internal memos in the ministries suggested that on at least one matter the outcome of the discussion had been less conclusive than the Protocol indicated.[40] While the Protocol gives us a good idea

THE VILLA, THE LAKE, THE MEETING

of Heydrich's message, it is thus less useful in identifying what role the other participants played at the meeting, and how they responded to what they heard. We can glean some clues, and others from post-war testimony, but that is all.

According to the Protocol,[41] Heydrich began by reminding his guests that Göring had entrusted him with preparing the Final Solution of the European Jewish question. The purpose of the present meeting was to establish clarity on fundamental questions. The Reich Marshal's desire to be provided with an outline of the organizational, policy and technical prerequisites for the Final Solution of the European Jewish question made it necessary to ensure in advance that the central organizations involved be brought together[42] and their policies properly coordinated. Overall control of the Final Solution lay, irrespective of geographical boundaries, with the Reichsführer SS and chief of the German police (i.e. Himmler) and specifically with Heydrich as his representative.

Heydrich then reminded his listeners of the recent history of Nazi action against the Jews. The principal goals had been to remove Jews from different sectors of German society and then from German soil. The only solution available at the time had been to accelerate Jewish emigration, a policy that led in 1939 to the creation of the Reich Central Office for Jewish Emigration. The disadvantages of a policy of emigration were clear to all those involved, he said, but in the absence of alternatives the policy had had to be tolerated, at least initially. But the Reichsführer SS had now stopped emigration in view of the dangers it raised during wartime and the new possibilities in the east.

Instead of emigration, Heydrich continued, the Führer had given his approval for a new kind of solution – the evacuation of Jews to the east. The next, ambiguous, sentence reads, 'These actions are nevertheless to be seen only as temporary relief [*Ausweichmöglich-keiten*] but they are providing the practical experience which is of great significance for the coming final solution of the Jewish question.' With breathtaking calmness, the minutes continue with the observation that around eleven million Jews would be affected by the Final Solution. A table was provided listing European countries and their Jewish populations. The list included not only those countries under German occupation or control (Part A), but also Germany's European allies, neutral countries, and those with whom it was still at war (Part B). These figures, Heydrich noted, had had to be drawn from the given statistics of religious affiliation, since the countries involved as yet lacked a proper racial census. Some rather motley remarks followed about the difficulty of tackling the Jewish question in Romania and Hungary and the occupational composition of Jews in Russia. Whether Eichmann's Protocol was just picking up fragments here, or Heydrich had been responding to questions, or his presentation really did offer these little snippets, we do not know. Then came one of the most significant sections of the Protocol:

In the course of the Final Solution and under appropriate leadership, the Jews should be put to work in the East. In large, single-sex labour columns, Jews fit to work will work their way eastwards constructing roads. Doubtless the large majority will be eliminated by natural causes. And doubtless any final remnant that survives will consist of the most resistant elements. They will have to be dealt with appropriately, because otherwise, by natural selection, they would form the germ cell of a new Jewish revival. (See the experience of history.)

Germany and the Czech Protectorate would have to be cleared first and then Europe would be combed from west to east. Bit by bit the Jews would be brought to transit ghettos and then sent further east.

Heydrich identified some key prerequisites for the deportations (or 'evacuations' in the language of the Protocol). There had to be clarity about who was going to be deported. Jews over sixty-five and those with serious war injuries or Iron Cross First Class would be sent to Theresienstadt. At a stroke this would obviate the many interventions on their behalf. The larger evacuation actions would commence when the military situation allowed. There followed discussion involving Martin Luther from the Foreign Office about the situation in countries allied to Germany or under its influence – Slovakia, Croatia, Italy, France and so on. South-eastern Europe and western Europe would raise no particular problems, Luther assured the other representatives, but caution should be taken in approaching the Scandinavian countries. In view of the small number of Jews involved, deferring Jewish measures in Scandinavia should not be a major problem.

A lengthy discussion of the issue of half-Jews and mixed marriages followed, taking up almost a third of the minutes. We will return to this shortly, since it undoubtedly constituted for Heydrich one of the most important topics of the day. At this stage let us note his proposal that so-called first-degree *Mischlinge* be evacuated to the east with the rest of the Jews. There would be a few exceptions, and in these cases the person concerned should be sterilized. For the SS Race and Settlement Office Hofmann argued that 'extensive use should be made of sterilisation; particularly as the Mischling, presented with the choice of evacuation, would rather submit to sterilisation'. As far as Jews in mixed marriages were concerned, Heydrich said that a decision should be made on the merits of each individual case as to whether the Jewish partner should be evacuated or, in view of the impact of such a measure on the German relatives, should be sent to an old-age ghetto.

The latter part of the minutes records a number of interventions from individual participants. Possibly the Protocol gathered up individual interjections that had been made at various points in the meeting and inserted them here. However, in cross-examination in Jerusalem Eichmann indicated that towards the end of the Wannsee meeting, and somewhat fortified by brandy, the participants turned what had been a monologue from Heydrich into a bit more of a free for all.[43] State Secretary Neumann from the Four-Year Plan organization said that Jews should not be removed from essential enterprises unless replacement labour could be provided. Heydrich agreed, pointing out that this was already the procedure. Dr Josef Bühler from the Generalgouvernement asked for the Final Solution to be begun in Poland, since transport was no major problem and there were no serious manpower issues to be borne in mind. The paraphrase of his argument in the Protocol continues:

The Jews must be removed from the territory of the Generalgouvernement as quickly as possible because of the particular danger there of epidemics being brought on by Jews. Jewish black-market activities were persistently destabilizing the region's economy. The 2½ million Jews in the region were in any case largely unable to work.

The authorities in the Generalgouvernement accepted Heydrich's primacy in the Jewish question, Bühler said, and would support his work. Bühler 'had only one request – that the Jewish question be solved as quickly as possible'.

An ominous section at the end of the Protocol noted that 'in conclusion the various possible kinds of solution were discussed'. A rather obscure sentence added that both Dr Meyer and Dr Bühler took the view that in the course of the Final Solution certain preparatory work should be carried out directly in the territories concerned,[44] though without alarming the populace. With a last request for cooperation and assistance in carrying out his tasks Heydrich closed the meeting. Afterwards, says Eichmann, the guests stood around in small groups for a little while, and then left.

Genocide, or what the Staatssekretäre learned

The Jews, learned the Staatssekretäre, were to be 'evacuated to the east'. Did this phrase mean the transportation of the Jewish population to a more easterly location? It is a staple of Holocaust deniers that it does. Serious historians, too, in questioning whether there was open talk about murder, have allowed doubt to arise whether Wannsee established that the Jews were to be killed. True, Eichmann said several times in Jerusalem that the language spoken on 20 January had been more open about killings than the Protocol suggests. Such an admission fitted in with Eichmann's defence strategy, which was to establish that his superiors had given clear killing orders.[45] The testimony of the ministerial bureaucrats at the Nuremberg Trials was very different. Their defence strategy was to claim they had known nothing of the Jews' fate, and they thus denied anything had been said openly.[46] Wilhelm Stuckart, having at first claimed barely to remember attending the conference, responded in cross examination:

No, I don't believe that I am wrong in saying that there was no discussion of the Final Solution of the Jewish Question, in the sense in which it is now understood.

KEMPNER: Heydrich related clearly, in your presence, what it was about?

STUCKART: That is absolutely out of the question – otherwise I would have known what it meant.[47]

Kritzinger from the Reich Chancellery was alone among Robert Kempner's post-war interviewees in expressing feelings of shame.[48] Yet he too denied killings had been openly talked about, a fact that has led eminent historians such as Hans Mommsen and Dieter Rebentisch to believe that this was the truth.[49] Stuckart's subordinate, Bernhard Lösener, by contrast, argued after the war that 'at the latest at the notorious Wannsee Conference ... Stuckart gained precise information'.[50]

There is a danger of two separate matters being confused here. One is the question whether the Wannsee Protocol clearly and explicitly envisaged the killing of all Jews. The other is whether the *means* of killing were clearly determined and articulated. On the former question, the evidence is straightforward. Otto Hofmann was sure that half-Jews could be relied upon to prefer sterilization if the alternative was 'evacuation'. Heydrich argued that because of the psychological impact on the German relatives the Jewish partner in mixed marriages might be deported to a ghetto rather than 'evacuated'. What kind of 'evacuation' could they be talking about? 'One thing is clear,' concluded the judges in the Ministries Trial at Nuremberg, 'no one would suggest sterilization as a procedure of amelioration unless he was wholly convinced that deportation meant a worse fate, namely, death.'[51]

But the Protocol is even more revealing than that. With ice-cold precision Heydrich clarified that Jews fit for work were all programmed to die. Either they would be crushed by working conditions or murdered for being resilient enough to survive them. The fate of Jews deemed *unable* to work at the outset could hardly be open to doubt. Bühler justified his request that the Final Solution begin in the Generalgouvernement with the argument that most of the Jews there were unable to work – another indication that the participants knew they were talking about murder.[52]

The Protocol suggests that a comprehensive plan was just emerging. Until then, Heydrich argued, almost everything had been provisional for want of something better. But the recent actions in the autumn had allowed invaluable experience to be gained. The planning process had matured and that was why it was necessary for the parties to come together prior to implementation of the Final Solution (as now defined). Those historians who believe a decision had been made long before have difficulty understanding Heydrich's statements and effectively have to discount them. But against the background of the crystallization of policy in autumn 1941, his comments make 'sense'. His statement that the existing deportations had been temporary relief adds credence to the idea that the deportations ordered in September had not yet been properly tied to a clear strategy for eliminating the Jews.

What reason is there to believe Christian Gerlach's view that the meeting's scope had been decisively widened, subsequent to the drawing up of the original invitation list, by a Hitler-decision in December to murder all European Jews? As already intimated in relation to the guest list, the evidence is not very conclusive. At his trial, Eichmann indicated that he had carried out the preparatory work for Heydrich's eventual speech in advance of the December deadline, and not in January. Eichmann said that he did the statistical work for Heydrich's broad survey of the European Jewish problem some two weeks before the original date.[53] Eichmann's references to dates are, of course, always to be approached with caution. We know he ordered the Reich Association for Jews to produce German statistics at the beginning of November and that he had already required European figures earlier in the summer, but it is hard to be certain about exactly what he put together for Heydrich and when.[54]

More significant is that in his Jerusalem testimony about Wannsee Eichmann made no reference to a Hitler-decision in December, though it would have been very much in his interest to do so. The Protocol itself says merely that new possibilities of 'evacuation' (i.e. murder) had emerged, not by Hitler's order, but merely with the Führer's 'prior approval'. This was clearly a reference to the deportation decisions in September 1941. Such a cautious and rather passive account of Hitler's role is no surprise in the written Protocol: it accorded with Hitler's desire not to be linked on paper to a murder order. But if Gerlach's emphasis on Hitler's decision of December 1941 were correct, we might have expected that orally at least Heydrich would have made stronger reference to the Führer's 'decision' – and certainly that at his trial Eichmann would have remembered it. After all, his own defence rested on the existence of unambiguous orders that he, as a mere underling, was simply carrying out. Yet Eichmann had nothing to say on the matter.[55] On balance, therefore, Heydrich had probably always planned to make a presentation with European dimensions, based on the decisions that had crystallized in October–November.

In another striking recent interpretation, the historian Peter Longerich has challenged the idea that Wannsee expressed a commitment to anything beyond the deportation programme unleashed by Hitler's decision in September 1941.[56] Longerich argues that the only difference was that it was now openly on the table that no one was designed to survive the deportations for long. Wannsee, he points out, was not followed by any immediate decision to expand the scale of the killing facilities. Instead, there was simply a notification from Eichmann that the deportations were to be resumed as soon as transport bottlenecks allowed. In short, for Longerich, Wannsee was simply an occasion for the murderous rhetoric surrounding the deportations to be ratcheted up a notch. Yet in September, as we have seen, Hitler's green light was quite probably still linked to the idea of an eastern reservation. The 'temporary' locations of Łódź or Minsk were holding bays before the populations could be sent further east the following spring. To be sure the whole process was already murderous enough, but that is different from explicit murder. By Wannsee it was clear all were to die. The reference to killing Jewish workers who survived the working conditions could scarcely have been more explicit. The 'eastern' territory to which the Jews should be evacuated was now mere code.

The only open question is about the means of killing. Did Wannsee take place at a time when the Nazi leadership, though now committed to deaths rather than a territorial solution of slow attrition, had not yet clearly established the *actual method* of killing? Had they still to establish the balance between gassing Jews, shooting them, or starving and working them to death? Or did the Protocol show, in fact, that a fair measure of clarity existed even here? There are some indications that Heydrich *did* talk at the meeting about how the Jews would be murdered. There is the ominous reference in the minutes to the discussion of the various 'forms of solution' (*Lösungsmöglichkeiten*). Possibly Bühler's comment that the transport issue would not be an impediment in the Generalgouvernement implied awareness that extermination camps were being developed in Poland and that deportations into distant parts of the Soviet Union were no longer being considered.[57] Given Heydrich's comments about Jewish workers, it is certainly hard to imagine that he had not anticipated and did not respond to questions about how the Jews would be killed. Eichmann said in Jerusalem that they discussed the 'business with the engine' and shooting, but not poison gas.[58] He may have been distinguishing here between killing using the internal combustion engine – the technique already employed at Chelmno – and cyanide, a method tried out at Auschwitz but not yet in general use.

Yet, there is no hard and fast proof that the participants learned at the meeting that Jews were going to be gassed. Kritzinger and Stuckart, as we know, denied hearing such talk. In an entry in his official diary made later in the war, Bühler's boss, Hans Frank, implied that it was only in the latter part of the war that he heard of the gassing of Jews. This diary is itself unreliable. From 1943 onwards Frank was mindful of being on the Allies' list of war criminals and conscious of the need to falsify the historical record.[59] After all, as far as we know, Frank had been involved in the discussions surrounding the construction of Bełżec in 1941. Nevertheless, some doubt about Wannsee must remain.

But the point is worth making again: whether or not the means were clearly established, the 'Final Solution' now unambiguously meant the death of all European Jews. Except for the specific 'privileged' exceptions to be deported to the old-age ghetto (at Theresienstadt – most of whom, as we know, were in any case sent on to Auschwitz), there was no other outcome than death. Possibly this was not spelled out at the meeting itself, but that is of only secondary importance; it was there, in black and white, in the Protocol. At the latest by the time it landed on their desks, Stuckart, Kritzinger and all the rest knew what it was that was being planned.[60] Small wonder that both Stuckart and Kritzinger's boss, Heinrich Lammers, denied having received it. Lammers's denial was undermined by the fact that, two years earlier, in 1946, he had freely acknowledged having read the document (it contained 'nothing new', he claimed at that point). Unfortunately for him the Protocol was then found by the Allies and its explosive contents exposed. Stuckart's denial was equally implausible, since he agreed to send a subordinate to a follow-up meeting, the invitations for which had arrived in the same post as the Protocol. But both men knew what they would be admitting, if they acknowledged receipt.[61]

Heydrich's remarks shed light on the evolution not just of the Final Solution but also of Nazi attitudes to Jewish labour. Some of the ambiguities of Nazi policy at this time reflect the fact that just as deportation plans were being replaced by murder, the authorities were being confronted with manpower shortages on a dangerous new scale.[62] Over the previous couple of years the use made of Jewish labour reserves had been extremely haphazard and contradictory. In the Generalgouvernement, lip service had been paid in many quarters to the idea of distinguishing between productive Jews and others, and this distinction became the rationale for ever more concrete proposals about eliminating those unfit for work. But even those

Jews designated as capable of working were not used effectively; payment, rations and discipline were so horrific as to prevent rational exploitation of labour. Working conditions on SS projects were an extended form of murder.[63]

In the Soviet Union policy had moved back and forth on the issue. The early approach of the Einsatzkommandos was to emphasize 'security' and disregard manpower, eliminating all Jewish men of working age. Exceptions were then introduced for key workers and the Wehrmacht made extensive use of Jewish labour. The pendulum began to swing back towards killing, however, and the security police/SS tried to restrict use of Jewish labour. Where Jewish workers were indispensable, Himmler's men sought to bring them under their own control and deploy them in separate work columns. Towards the end of 1941, in answer to various inquiries, we thus find the Ministry for the Eastern Territories informing its subordinates that in principle economic considerations should be disregarded in eliminating Jews. But manpower shortages were becoming more acute again, and there was renewed pressure to conserve labour. Shootings reduced in number for a while because of the critical manpower shortage.[64]

One attempt to square the circle of needing Jews and wanting to get rid of them can be seen in the emergence of an explicit concept of extermination through labour. Starting in the Soviet Union, the Einsatzgruppe C developed the idea of using Jews for construction projects, in a way that would solve temporary labour shortages and at the same time wear out and kill the workers. In Galicia, SSPF Katzmann developed the idea of employing Jewish workers under literally murderous conditions to reconstruct a major transit route.[65] Himmler himself began to think more actively about using Jewish labour in the concentration camps, and in January 1942 he prepared the concentration camps for a major influx of Jewish labour (which only partially materialized). It is against this background that we can understand Heydrich's remarks. Echoing Katzmann's lethal project, Heydrich attempted to balance recognition of current labour scarcities with the desire to eliminate all Jews.[66] It is possible, as Hans

Mommsen has argued, that the fiction of rationally utilizing labour provided the psychological function of creating a bridge from the reservation policy to that of genocide.[67] But if Heydrich ever had needed such a psychological bridge, his willingness to kill off competent and resilient workers suggested that he had already crossed the Rubicon.

Controlling the boundaries

The Wannsee conference is thus a kind of keyhole, through which we can glimpse the emerging Final Solution. It took place at a time when the idea of a reservation had been abandoned, labour scarcities were pressing, and when the Nazis may or may not have decided exactly how to eliminate all the Jews. But it is evident that Wannsee is not the place at which the murder decisions themselves were taken. For the most part, Heydrich was disseminating conclusions drawn elsewhere. On some issues the participants had something to say; for the most part their role was to listen and to nod.

Why then had he called them together? One of the few areas where there were still clear differences of principle, particularly between the ministries and the RSHA, was the question of how to deal with the borderline cases of half-Jews and mixed marriages.[68] The Interior Ministry felt in advance of the meeting that this was likely to be the key item on the agenda. Even after the war, State Secretary Stuckart still claimed that Heydrich had called the meeting primarily to remove obstacles to deporting half-Jews and Jews in mixed marriages.[69]

The problem of defining who was a Jew had faced the Nazis ever since they came to power. Early measures, such as the forced retirement of civil servants in 1933, used a broad definition, targeting those with even one Jewish grandparent. Party members had to prove the absence of Jewish forebears back to 1800, SS officials back to 1750. With the reintroduction of conscription in 1935, however, the army was allowed to make 'exceptions' and recruit half- and quarter-Jewish recruits – which it seems to have done with alacrity.

Party radicals were worried that precedents were being set that might lead to civil rights for half- and quarter-Jews. Their pressure for a definitive and far-reaching ruling helps explain Hitler's decision to announce citizenship and blood laws, the so-called Nuremberg Laws, at the Party rally in Nuremberg in September 1935.[70]

The history of the Nuremberg Laws, and particularly of the subsequent decrees establishing their precise scope, revealed that unlike 'full Jews', half- and quarter-Jews had institutional champions, above all Stuckart's department in the Ministry of the Interior, with assistance from the Reich Chancellery. Why the Interior Ministry should have played this role is not clear. It may well have reflected a particular commitment on the part of Bernhard Lösener, Stuckart's expert on Jewish questions. Whatever the original motivation, once the Interior Ministry took on the half-Jewish cause, ministerial prestige was at stake. Even Lösener's own post-war testimony, in which he was at pains to underline his anti-Nazi credentials, makes evident that the issue became as much a question of departmental *amour propre* as of moral principle.[71]

The other factor helping the *Mischlinge* was Hitler's sensitivity to public morale. There were so many full-German relatives to consider. Ideologically, Hitler favoured the hard line of the Party radicals, but tactically he was very hesitant.[72] A classic example is his behaviour in relation to the Nuremberg Laws. The Interior Ministry sought to add a clause stating that 'These Laws apply to Full Jews only'. Hitler allowed the amendment to be included in the press release announcing the Laws, but had it deleted at the same time from the actual legal text.[73] His role was equally equivocal in the long-drawn-out battle of definitions that followed promulgation of the Laws.

The Party radicals were by and large willing to accept the quarter-Jew, but wanted to see half-Jews designated as Jews, with a few exceptions individually sanctioned by the Party. The Interior Ministry, by contrast, argued that the half-German should be protected rather than the half-Jew being punished.[74] The compromise outcome was a new legal category, the '*Mischling*', defined by a disparate muddle of religious and 'racial' criteria. Quarter-Jews were termed

'*Mischlinge*'[75] but allowed to marry other Germans, though not other *Mischlinge* or Jews. Half-Jews were also considered *Mischlinge* unless they were members of synagogues or had married a Jew, in which case they were considered Jews (the so-called '*Geltungs-juden*').[76] The Party's desire to be able to select which (few) half-Jews might be tolerated had failed, but so had the Interior Ministry's blanket protection of the half-Jew. Moreover, the radicals succeeded in introducing a ruling that half-Jews were forbidden from marrying quarter-Jews or Germans, unless exceptions were allowed by Hitler. The only way they could maintain their status as *Mischlinge* was thus either to stay single or to marry another half-Jew.[77]

The other key boundary issue was that of mixed marriages. The Nuremberg Laws, though banning future unions between Jews and non-Jews, had had little to say about existing mixed marriages. At the end of 1938, however, after consulting Hitler, Göring drew up guidelines, distinguishing between so-called 'privileged mixed marriage' and the others. The privileged marriages were those where the man was non-Jewish, with the exception of marriages where there were Jewishly educated children. Marriages in which the husband was Jewish were not privileged, with the exception of those marriages in which there were Christian children (and the children were still living or had fallen in active service). If the Jewish partner was the wife, then the new controls on Jewish property affected her property only. When the Yellow Star was introduced, the privileged marriages were extended to include Jews married to second-degree *Mischlinge*, and even Jews whose marriages had been terminated by divorce or death, provided they were the parents of a *Mischling* child (or had been and the child had been killed in action). Jews in such privileged marriages did not have to wear the star. The bizarre mixture of 'racial', religious and gendered criteria, lacking any theoretical rationale, shows how dominant was the regime's fear of public reaction.[78]

In 1941 the Party radicals renewed efforts to extend their definitional power and remove the protected categories. A working group was formed by members of Walter Gross's Racial Policy

Office and the new Institute for Research on the Jewish Question in Frankfurt, calling for *Mischlinge* to be legally equated with Jews.[79] The RSHA too began to take a more active interest, particularly once it became important to define which groups should be deported from the Reich. On 21 August 1941 Eichmann convened a meeting at which the Party Chancellery, the Racial Policy Office and the RSHA coordinated their demands. The demands raised were almost exactly those Heydrich put on the table at Wannsee.[80]

With one or two exceptions,[81] Heydrich had invited to the meeting all parties involved in decisions on half- and quarter-Jews – or *Mischlinge* first and second degree, as they were known. Heydrich now mounted a frontal assault on the compromises erected since the Nuremberg Laws. First-degree *Mischlinge* were to be equated with full Jews. Only those with proven, exceptional service for state and Party behind them, or possessing children who were second-degree *Mischlinge*, could hope for better treatment. The best they could hope for was 'voluntary' sterilization. Even in relation to the second-degree *Mischlinge*, Heydrich's proposals breached the general understanding of protection. Where, for example, both parents were *Mischlinge* first degree, where they *looked* racially particularly unfavourable, or where there was a particularly negative police or political record, they could be treated as Jews. The latter case would not apply if the second-degree *Mischlinge* had married a German partner, but offered considerable scope for widespread deportation. Heydrich was equally radical on mixed marriages. Now, all Jewish partners of German spouses were destined for deportation. The only choice for the authorities would be between evacuation, i.e. murder, or deportation to an old-age ghetto. Where half-Jews were married to Germans, evacuation or deportation to an old-age ghetto of the half-Jews would occur unless there were children who had been deemed second-degree *Mischlinge*, in which case the parent would stay.[82]

The numbers at stake were small. There were fewer than 20,000 mixed marriages in Germany.[83] According to Lösener, in 1939 there were 64,000 first-degree and 43,000 second-degree *Mischlinge* in the

Old Reich, Austria and the Sudeten area.[84] True, there were many more non-German *Mischlinge* in other parts of Europe, but Heydrich probably had little fear that they would remain 'untouchable'. After all, no one was worried about the morale of those married or related to Jews *outside* Germany; the argument that *Mischlinge* were half-German also did not apply. So Heydrich's assault was not about numbers and all about asserting total definitional power under the banner of a radical concept of race. The purpose of Wannsee was to reinforce the RSHA's pre-eminence in all aspects of the Jewish question.

Securing compliance and complicity

A number of historian have seen in Heydrich's actions above all a personal initiative to maintain or demonstrate his power.[85] Wolfgang Scheffler, for example, has pointed out that Heydrich did not control the concentration camps, and thus that a growing empire lay outside his jurisdiction. Wannsee was his attempt to reassert a declining position.[86] But when we bear in mind that Heydrich was then in charge of the Czech Protectorate, with a magnificent official residence in Prague, and that he had been entrusted with masterminding an enormous deportation programme, bringing him into contact with authorities all over Europe, it is hard to believe he was fearful of loss of authority. By contrast, Eberhard Jäckel has argued that Wannsee was a ceremonial event, designed to show that Heydrich had come out from Himmler's shadow. This gains some credence from Eichmann's post-war testimony. 'The prime motive for Heydrich himself,' Adolf Eichmann said in Jerusalem, 'was doubtless to expand his power and authority.' Elsewhere Eichmann spoke of Heydrich 'indulging his well-known vanity – that was his weakness, showing off a mandate which made him the master of Jews in all the areas occupied and influenced by Germany and thus demonstrating his enhanced influence'.[87] Heydrich's choice of the stylish villa on the Wannsee lake adds to our sense that he was playing gesture politics.[88]

Yet the conference was not really about vanity. Instead, it was part of a concerted, coordinated campaign by Himmler and Heydrich to assert their supremacy. Heydrich's invitation, his opening remarks at the meeting, and indeed his follow-up letter to the conference, at which he expressed pleasure that 'happily the basic line was established as regards the practical execution of the Final Solution of the Jewish question',[89] all indicate that a major aim was to achieve unity and common purpose among the participants, and above all to secure acceptance of the RSHA's leading role. Two weeks before the Wannsee invitations went out, both Himmler and Heydrich had arranged a series of meetings. In mid-November Himmler and Rosenberg had their lengthy confabulation.[90] A day later Himmler and Heydrich conferred to coordinate their policy on, among other things, 'Eliminating the Jews'.[91] On 24 November it was Wilhelm Stuckart's turn to confer with Himmler. Number three of the four points in Himmler's appointments calendar was 'Jewish question – belongs to me'.[92] If the post-war testimony of Bernhard Lösener is to be believed, Stuckart complained in the following weeks that Jewish matters were being taken away from the ministry. On 28 November Himmler had yet another meeting on the issue – this time conferring with the HSSPF of the Generalgouvernement, Friedrich-Wilhelm Krüger, to discuss the obstacles Governor Frank was putting in the way of 'central management of Jewish questions'.[93] Between the invitation and the eventual Wannsee conference there were more such encounters, most notably between Himmler and Bühler on 13 January.

Himmler and Heydrich were thus making strenuous efforts to coordinate and centralize all initiatives on the Jewish question. Given the widespread support for anti-Jewish measures, we might wonder why this was necessary. The defence attorney in Jerusalem asked Eichmann whether Heydrich had any real reason to fear opposition. Eichmann's reply was instructive:

According to the practice until then, all the offices were always trying, for departmental reasons, to delay things and make reservations – in other words, there was always a whole series of individual discussions in the long-drawn-out deliberations held until then. Those were dragging on, and there was never a clear-cut solution achieved right away. This was the reason why Heydrich convened this Wannsee Conference, in order, as it were, to press through, on the highest level, his will and the will of the Reichsführer-SS and Chief of the German Police.[94]

Heydrich's real target was the civilian ministries – the other participants were brought along to strengthen his hand. In the weeks and months before the conference, Himmler and Heydrich had repeatedly clashed with civilian agencies over issues of competence. Both within Germany and in the occupied territories the demarcation lines were ill-defined. In autumn 1941 Heydrich's security police experienced regular run-ins with the Ministry for the Eastern Territories and particularly with the ministry's commissioners in the Baltic and White Russia. In early November, for example, Rudolf Lange, the head of Einsatzkommando 2 and Riga KdS who attended the Wannsee conference, had angry exchanges with the Reich Commissioner for Ostland, Hinrich Lohse, about the forthcoming deportations to Riga.[95]

In Poland the conflicts between Himmler's staff and the civilian administration were if anything even more intense. In May 1940 Governor Frank had stated unambiguously that the police were an enforcement arm of the government, though in practice he was never able to impose this view. A few days later, HSSPF Krüger complained to Himmler that the elevation to Staatssekretär rank of Frank's deputy, Josef Bühler, would mean that Krüger would have to take orders from the younger Bühler. Krüger was duly promoted to Staatssekretär, too.[96] In the period 1940 to 1941 Frank was involved in a continual battle to prevent Heydrich from deporting Jews from the Reich to the Generalgouvernement.

Other ministries, particularly the Interior Ministry, also had a contested relationship with the RSHA. Nominally, Himmler was the subordinate of the Minister of the Interior. In practice, Minister Frick had abandoned any pretence at controlling Himmler; indeed was giving up hope even of being informed of what the RSHA was up to.[97] Yet some jealously guarded questions of prerogative remained, particularly the borderline of mixed-race Jews. Alone among the civilian representatives at Wannsee, probably only Martin Luther from the Foreign Ministry had already resigned himself to subordination and had adapted by trying to be as helpful to the RSHA as possible. It is perfectly possible that Himmler and Heydrich could have resolved demarcation issues on an individual basis with each agency. The series of November meetings suggests they were in the process of doing so. Yet, in the complicated power structure of the Third Reich, a collective acknowledgement among all the interested parties was of much greater worth in establishing power and precedents. What is more, in the climate of a high-level meeting with a strong Party–SS presence, the other representatives would be much more susceptible to group pressure.

There was another aspect to the meeting: Heydrich wanted to establish shared complicity. 'The significant part from Heydrich's point of view,' Eichmann claimed in Jerusalem, 'was to nail down the Secretaries of State, to commit them most bindingly, to catch them by their words.'[98] The events around the transport of Berlin Jews to Riga on 29/30 November had brought to a head the growing disquiet flowing back to Berlin from a variety of sources over the treatment of the German-Jewish deportees and particularly following the first mass murders in Kovno and then in Riga. The knowledge of these shootings soon did the rounds in the Berlin authorities; Bernhard Lösener claimed in his case that they represented a personal turning point. Both Heydrich and Himmler were undoubtedly concerned to bind in all agencies to their enterprise and prevent further murmurings. The last thing they wanted was for Hitler to worry about morale and once again rein in their activities. Moreover, with the first premonitions in December that Germany might not win the war, establishing common complicity was a powerful force to ensure that other agencies toed the line. It would encourage them to hand over responsibility to the RSHA to avoid taking on further responsibility. We know, for example, that Otto Bräutigam, who represented the Ministry for the Eastern Territories at one of the follow-up conferences after Wannsee, concluded in January that Germany could not win the war. At a meeting on 29 January he showed an ostentatious willingness to make concessions to Heydrich's men. 'As far as the Jewish question was concerned,' he confided to one of his own colleagues, 'he was quite happy to emphasize the responsibility of the SS and the police.'[99]

Heydrich's aim of establishing shared knowledge of murder explains one of the real oddities of the Wannsee Protocol, namely its peculiar juxtaposition of euphemism and undisguised murderousness. On the one hand, it is coy about killing and talks of 'evacuation to the east'. On the other hand, the language about eliminating Jewish workers is so open, and the implications for the rest so clear, as to render the euphemisms useless as a disguise. The natural tendency of the RSHA was to be extremely guarded. The euphemisms were its normal mode of communicating about murder, and will have served here to remind recipients of the language codes they should use. At the same time it was so vital to establish the participants' shared knowledge in the killing programme that this overrode the need for caution. This was why Lammers, Stuckart and others were at such pains after the war to deny having seen the Protocol, to escape from the trap that Heydrich had set them.

Participating in genocide

It was the 'first time in my life', recalled Adolf Eichmann, that he had taken part 'in such a Conference in which ... senior officials participated, such as Secretaries of State – it was conducted very quietly and with much courtesy, with much friendliness – politely and nicely, there was not much speaking and it did not last a long time, the waiters served cognac, and in this way it ended'.[100] Even if not itself the deciding moment, Wannsee remains a powerfully symbolic one. These were not the barbarian hordes of some primitive people, pouring across the frontiers and slaughtering all who lay in their path. Here was the distinguished ambience of an elegant villa, in a cultivated suburb, in one of Europe's most sophisticated capitals. Here were fifteen educated, civilized bureaucrats, from an educated, civilized society, observing all due decorum. And here was genocide, going through, on the nod.

How could they have gone along with this? Did they believe in what they were doing? Or were they driven by secondary motives – competition for power perhaps, or blind obedience to duty? Or were they merely weakly complying with a process over which they had no control?

The first part of an answer must be that a surprising number of clever men round the table were true believers, for whom racist-nationalism was at the heart of their philosophy. These were by and large convinced Nazis and not dutiful functionaries. The fact that so many of the senior men were so young was a sign that newcomers had managed to rise rapidly into positions of power. This was particularly true in the SS and Party institutions but in the government ministries, too, long-term Nazis had climbed speedily up the ranks. New ministries, such as Rosenberg's Ministry for the Eastern Territories, Goebbels's Propaganda Ministry (not represented at Wannsee) or the civilian administration in Poland, contained very little of a pre-existing civil service ethos and were stuffed full of Party men. Alfred Meyer, for example, had joined the Nazi Party in 1928 and was a convinced Nazi – he had become gauleiter in Westphalia and a senior SA man years before he entered Rosenberg's ministry. His ministerial colleague Georg Leibbrandt had maintained contact with the Party since 1930. In the Polish administration, Josef Bühler owed his position to his long-established personal contacts with Hans Frank in whose legal practice he had worked in the 1920s.[101]

Even in the longer-established ministries, there had been ample opportunity for convinced Nazis to rise rapidly in their profession. Indeed, the longest-serving Nazi Party member round the table at Wannsee was to be found in the Justice Ministry, Roland Freisler, who joined the Party in 1925. Even before joining, Freisler, a decorated First World War veteran, had combined his legal practice with being a city deputy for the right-wing radical Völkisch-Sozialen

Block. After 1925 he was the Nazis' legal adviser in Kassel and in 1932 became an outspoken Nazi deputy in the Prussian parliament. Within months of the Nazi seizure of power, he was promoted rapidly up the Justice Ministry ladder to the position of Staatssekretär first in Prussia then at Reich level.[102] Wilhelm Stuckart was of a similar stamp. Having fought with the Freikorps in the civil war and been a member of the radical right-wing student body, the Skalden-Orden, like Freisler he became a legal adviser to the Nazi Party in the 1920s. In the 1930s he rose rapidly to high rank in the SS. His fast-track promotion to departmental chief in the Interior Ministry in 1935 owed not a little to his Party contacts. Stuckart personified a new generation of Staatssekretär – talented and highly qualified, capable of doing well under any circumstances, but nevertheless ideologically committed to the Nazi Party.[103]

Some of those appointed were undoubtedly not up to the job. Rosenberg's staff were particularly notorious in this regard: Meyer was by general account 'too weak to be good, too cowardly to sin',[104] and Leibbrandt, whose previous post had been head of the Eastern Section in the AA, was, like his master, Rosenberg, a fanatic and not particularly competent.[105] But generally speaking we need to wrest ourselves from the stereotype of the neutral educated bureaucrat, assiduously fulfilling the orders of the ignorant, irrational Nazi. It remains one of the most striking characteristics of Wannsee that most of the best educated round the table were also long-standing Nazis. Of the eight people who had doctorates, six were either 'old fighters' of the Nazi Party[106] or had at least enjoyed close contacts with the Party well before 1933.[107] The other two had long years of right-wing *völkisch*-national politics behind them: Rudolf Lange had belonged to the Burschenschaft Germania, while Gerhard Klopfer had been a member of the Deutscher Hochschulring.[108] Here was powerful evidence of the degree to which radical nationalist ideas had made substantial inroads into Germany's educated youth even before 1933.

In some cases bonds of friendship and shared ideas bridged the different institutions – the most striking being that between the SD's chief architect, Werner Best (not himself present at Wannsee), the Party man Gerhard Klopfer, and the civil servant Wilhelm Stuckart. In autumn 1941 these men founded a new journal, *Reich – Volksordnung – Lebensraum* (Reich – ethnic order – living space), for 'ethnically based [*völkisch*] constitution and administration'.[109] Men like Stuckart or Freisler were as deeply persuaded by Nazi ethnic-racial power politics as the Party officials or the men in the RSHA. Though not a rabid anti-Semite[110] in 1935 Freisler had published the article 'The tasks of the Reich justice system, proceeding from a biological standpoint'. The racial imperatives governing the state's activity emerged even more clearly a year later in his essay, 'The protection of race and racial stock in the emerging German legal system' in which he argued that the racial mixing of the previous centuries had to be reversed.[111]

In short, ideas really mattered at Wannsee. Yet when we look at the process by which these men had edged towards genocide, it is clear that there was no simple translation of ideas into politics. For one thing, there were opportunists round the table as well as ideologues. Heydrich's chief henchman, Heinrich Müller, for example, had before 1933 been a loyal servant of the Weimar state. It was his competence in the Munich police force that led Himmler and Heydrich to take him on to their staff, where he became a prime advocate of 'preventive law enforcement', attacking the regime's enemies before they committed a crime.[112] In 1937, opposing Heydrich's (ultimately successful) efforts to promote 'Gestapo Müller' further, the Munich Gauleitung recognized Müller's efforts combating the left:

It must be acknowledged that he fought them extremely vigorously [*äußerst scharf*], at times flouting legal restrictions. But it is equally clear that had it been his allotted task to do so, Müller would have been equally vigorous against the right. With his enormous ambition and drive he would have achieved the recognition of whatever superiors he was working for.[113]

At the heart of the RSHA and one of the most feared men in Germany, Müller was nevertheless one of the very last members round the Wannsee table to join the Nazi Party – he did so only in 1938.

Martin Luther joined the Nazis a little ahead of the seizure of power, in 1932, but was above all an entrepreneur and an opportunist, or as Walter Schellenberg from the RSHA put it, energetic but 'governed solely by the calculation of the businessman'.[114] With a successful business career behind him, he owed his rise in the Foreign Ministry above all to the fact that he had become a general factotum for Joachim von Ribbentrop and his wife in the 1930s, and had followed Ribbentrop into the ministry. When Luther entered the Foreign Office in 1938 he asked for jurisdiction over Party affairs but wanted Jewish matters left with another department. There is thus no basis for Gerald Reitlinger's suggestion that Luther made ' "anti-semitism his life's work" '.[115] On the contrary, he made the running in Jewish matters only later, when it seemed the means to assure the Foreign Office some continued influence at a time when its scope for activity was waning.[116] The example of Luther and Müller thus shows us that opportunism, or a desire for order, or simply not asking questions about the validity of the tasks assigned, could be mechanisms for encouraging participation.

Even more significant than naked opportunism, however, was that all the Wannsee participants, even those with a strong racial vision, had moved astonishingly far from what they might have imagined, even just a few years earlier. Wilhelm Stuckart's theoretical position on the Jews evolved markedly from the late 1930s to the early 1940s. Initially arguing that Jews were not inferior, only different, by 1942 he asserted that their lower quality justified their extermination.[117] He may well have assumed, in the 1930s, that the Jewish problem would be solved by emigration.[118] In the 1930s, Heydrich and Eichmann, too, had assumed, as revealed in position papers and memoranda since 1935, that the Jewish problem was above all one of emigration. If we can trust the sources, several leading members even of the SD were taken aback by the violence of the Kristallnacht pogrom, a pogrom they had not initiated.[119] Striking though the degree is to which educated young men subscribed to Nazi ideas, the fact is that they nevertheless embarked on a journey that left far behind what they could have imagined.

The earlier chapters have outlined in general terms some of the forces impelling them. At the centre of the process was Hitler, setting the tone, prescribing the boundaries, licensing every radical action, and spanning a rhetorical canopy that could shelter the most brutal of actions. More than anything or anyone else, it was he who shaped the pace and direction of the journey his men had travelled. It was his signals that had brought anti-Semitism to the centre of the SD's agenda or that had prompted the Interior Ministry's chipping away at Jewish citizenship rights for the best part of a decade.

In this evolving context, all the Wannsee participants adapted and responded. Some of them played a major role in the process, others were more carried along than leading. Some were enthusiastic, others less so, a diversity of response that reflected both pre-existing disposition and the pressures and opportunities associated with the particular offices held. The advance guard round the table was unquestionably formed by the men from the RSHA. All the civilian representatives felt under increasing pressure from Himmler and Heydrich. Even in the 1930s, in the melding of bureaucratic efficiency and radical ideology, Himmler and beneath him Heydrich had made a central contribution. During the 1930s, they, more than any other figures, had insinuated radical ideology into the state apparatus. By holding the concentration camps and the SS outside the state system Himmler had posed a permanent threat to help bring the bureaucracy into line.[120] After 1938, far more than other Wannsee participants, it was Heydrich who was the pace-setter on the Jewish question. It was he who masterminded the forced-emigration policy from Vienna and Berlin, he who superintended the deportations after the outbreak of war, he who drafted the increasingly murderous guidelines for the Einsatzgruppen in the Sudetenland, Poland and Russia. His direct subordinate, 'Gestapo Müller', had a hand in almost every facet of Jewish persecution. Below Müller, Adolf Eichmann, the man who made the arrangements for the Wannsee conference, would prove indefatigable as the orchestrator of deportations, as the cajoler of Jewish administrations all across Europe, tricking and threatening them into cooperating with genocide.

Probably the least committed to the genocidal project, and the most hesitant at trying to keep up with the RSHA's pace, was Friedrich Kritzinger. Born in 1890 and the oldest person present, he represented the shrinking group of bureaucrats who still embodied something of an older civil service ethos. Kritzinger and Erich Neumann from the Ministry of Economics/Four-Year Plan were the two civilian representatives at Wannsee who had joined the Nazi Party only after the Nazi seizure of power – in Kritzinger's case well after and clearly without enthusiasm. Neumann, a talented administrator with a successful career in the Prussian civil service behind him, joined both Party and SS only in 1933, and in 1942 would leave public service and enter the business world. But Neumann had been caught up in the atmosphere of the Four-Year Plan organization and was the loyal servant of the extremely anti-Semitic Göring. By contrast, the Reich Chancellery, to which Kritzinger had been recruited in 1938 as a competent and approachable administrator, was one of the few ministries small and cohesive enough to have sustained something of its pre-Nazi values.[121]

Though the Reich Chancellery was not itself responsible for initiating measures, its importance had increased markedly in the period after 1938, above all because of the access to Hitler enjoyed by its chief, Heinrich Lammers (a privilege which lasted until the end of 1943 when Martin Bormann blocked the gateway). Kritzinger, the unquestioned number two in the ministry, was party to many administrative decisions that were illegal even by the legal code then in force.[122] Yet there were a number of occasions on which he used his influence to slow down measures, particularly if they had implications for those Jews whom the department had identified as not beyond help – those in privileged mixed marriages and the *Mischlinge*. In 1940–41, for example, Kritzinger successfully opposed the Interior Ministry's proposal to declare German Jews stateless and thus 'protectees' (*Schutzangehörige*) of the Reich. Kritzinger asserted at Nuremberg with justice that he had been no hardliner (*Scharfmacher*). 'What incriminates him,' wrote the historian Hans Mommsen in an expert report about Kritzinger in the 1960s, 'is less his occasional initiative than his weakness.'[123] Even on the issue of the *Mischlinge*, the Reich Chancellery eventually felt it had to give ground to the radicals. It was Lammers who in autumn 1941 gave approving nods to the idea of sterilizing all *Mischlinge* – at a time when the Interior Ministry was still resisting such measures.

Overall, the civilian ministries with domestic responsibilities within German had no direct responsibility for killing. They made murder much easier, however, by moving with the tide and refining and consolidating the legal foundations for the expropriation and segregation of Germany's Jews. On 20 April 1940, to take just one of countless examples, Stuckart wrote to the Ministerial Council for Reich Defence on the matter of the treatment of Jewish forced labour under German labour laws. Stuckart had noticed that Jews affected by works closures on New Year's Day, Easter Monday, Whit Monday or Christmas Day were enjoying paid holidays. On his own initiative, Stuckart recommended that Jews be excluded from remuneration.[124] An even more sinister move on his part, to declare Jews stateless and thus 'Protectees of the Reich', was motivated by the recognition that the Ministry of the Interior was losing all control over deportations to the RSHA. He thus wanted to absolve the ministry of legal responsibility for deported Jews.[125] (This particular initiative was frustrated by the Reich Chancellery and by Hitler's subsequent dictum that legislation on citizenship was irrelevant since after the war there would be no Jews in Germany.[126]) Yet even Stuckart, for all his intellectual kinship with Klopfer and Best, was still to some extent influenced by a moral climate different from that in Heydrich's RSHA.[127] After Kritzinger, he was probably the person who came to the Wannsee table with the most reservations, above all because of his department's attempts to protect half-Jews and Jews in mixed marriages.

In the course of 1941 an increasing number of those round the table had been in one way or another initiated into murder. The representatives of the Ministry for the Eastern Territories were well acquainted with it. In October they sent instructions out to the commissioners in the field that there were no objections to eliminating

Jews who could not work.[128] By mid-November they were arguing that economic considerations should not figure in the elimination of the 'problem'.[129] For his part, anyone with as much power and influence in the Generalgouvernement as Josef Bühler could not fail to know a great deal about killing Jews. His civilian subordinates had shaped ration-allocations and wage-scales in such a way that Jews had the choice of illegally obtaining food or dying. In December Bühler had been privy to his boss Hans Frank's speech, calling for the Jews of the Generalgouvernement to be done away with in one way or another.

Ministries and agencies with no direct contact to the killing fields were also increasingly well informed. For on thing, the Einsatzgruppen in Russia produced regular detailed accounts about the numbers they had killed, and the distribution list for the summary reports was progressively expanded. We know that Martin Bormann in the Party Chancellery received copies, so his representative at Wannsee, Klopfer, will probably have seen them as well.[130] In October 1941 the Gestapo chief Heinrich Müller distributed the first five reports to the German department in the Foreign Office. From the third one on it was clear to the recipients that Jews were being killed quite separately from partisans.[131] By the end of 1941 the mass murder of Soviet Jews was very widely known within the Foreign Office.[132] It is possible, but not certain, that in the winter of 1941 the Reich Chancellery also received these documents.[133] In the Interior Ministry, too, the facts were coming out. Bernhard Lösener, Stuckart's deputy, described after the war hearing from another official the fate of the Berlin deportees to Riga.[134] Confronting Stuckart with this information (if Lösener's account is to be trusted) he was met with the reply, ' "Don't you know that these things are ordered at the highest level?" '[135]

What is striking is how many people round the table had given direct killing orders or themselves had experience of killing. It was Heydrich's apparatus that set the pace in murder. The SS/SD leaders, Heydrich and Müller, directed the killing operations of the Einsatzgruppen. Heydrich may well have experienced Einsatzgruppen killings at first hand; he had certainly been in the field around the time of Einsatzgruppen murders and given orders for them to be intensified, as, for example, in Grodno at the end of June 1941.[136] We know that his boss, Himmler, attended a mass shooting in August. In September or October 1941, according to his later testimony, Adolf Eichmann witnessed a mass shooting in Minsk.[137] Shortly before this, Eichmann had called for the Jews of Serbia to be shot. The security chiefs in the Generalgouvernement and the Riga district, Schöngarth and Lange, arrived dripping with blood: Lange had led the Einsatzkommando 2 in Riga and had been responsible for shooting the Jews of Riga at the end of November 1941; Schöngarth had created the special Einsatzgruppe to carry out murders in the Galician territory. As BdS of the Generalgouvernement it was he who in November 1941 introduced the so-called *Schießbefehl* (shooting order), which allowed Jews found outside the ghetto areas to be summarily shot.[138] In September 1941 Martin Luther from the Foreign Ministry approached Heydrich unsolicited, seeking his support for shooting Serbian Jews rather than deporting them.[139] His subordinate Franz Rademacher visited Serbia to determine conditions on the ground, where he found that the army was already 'solving' the problem. Christopher Browning argues that it was Luther's energy and devotion to the cause that 'earned' the Foreign Office a place at the Wannsee table.[140] The oft-cited gap between the 'desk murderers' and the men in the field barely applies at Wannsee.

It was thus small wonder that nobody had declined to attend the meeting on principle. No one arrived at Wannsee with even the faintest intention of speaking up for the Jews. In the pressured atmosphere, with such a strong corps of supporters from the RSHA, the SS and the Party, Heydrich was able to push forward with little opposition, even on the contested *Mischling* question. Only the borderline cases enjoyed any defence at all – the privilege of sterilization. Only Jews essential for German production should enjoy a temporary reprieve. No one raised objections to the proposals for murder. It was much too late for that.

5

A largely successful day

Did Heydrich get what he wanted at Wannsee? The Protocol suggests the RSHA achieved two breakthroughs. First, the age-old conflict with the civilian authorities in the Generalgouvernement over the Jewish question seemed to have ended. Josef Bühler, according to the Protocol, had actively invited the RSHA to begin the Final Solution there. The foundations for this new accord had already been laid in December, when Hans Frank had met Hitler and gained an inkling of future plans, and in January, when Bühler had met Himmler and left the meeting very satisfied. Whereas in previous years the RSHA had treated the Generalgouvernement as the 'rubbish tip' of the Reich, now it was promising to carry out ethnic cleansing. Removing Jews *from* the Generalgouvernement by whatever means, rather than dumping them *on* the region, was something on which the RSHA and Bühler could agree. In fact, demarcation disputes would continue, though Frank was to suffer some decisive reversals in the course of the year. But all Bühler was interested in now was the speed with which the security police would be able to do away with the Jews.[1]

Even more striking were the signs that Staatssekretär Stuckart had buckled. It was predictable that SS-Gruppenführer Hofmann, speaking for the SS Race and Settlement Office, should have echoed Heydrich's arguments about the *Mischlinge*. Less expected was Stuckart's response. Having anticipated an assault from Heydrich, his expert on Jewish matters, Lösener, had produced yet another paper outlining the reasons why the *Mischlinge* should be protected.[2] But instead of holding the ministry's line, Stuckart now – according to the Protocol – proposed the compulsory sterilization of all *Mischlinge*. His stance on mixed marriages was even more radical. Complaining about the administrative work involved in separating Jewish partners from their spouses, he called for a simple legislative act 'such that the law in effect says: "These marriages have been dissolved."' This would facilitate the deportation of the Jews. Why did Stuckart give way? The most generous interpretation is that he was in fact playing a clever game. At Nuremberg he did not deny having taken this position, but claimed that he had been seeking to deflect the 'evacuations' and had thought sterilization would prove in practice not to be feasible.[3] In the view of his subordinate Lösener and another former official in the Ministry of the Interior, Hans Globke, Stuckart had received information from State Secretary Dr Leonardo Conti that mass sterilization was not practicable during wartime (a fact that subsequent meetings indeed confirmed).[4] Stuckart said, according to Lösener, that he was attempting delaying tactics and hoped at the end of the war for a 'noble gesture'.[5] This is possible, but two points speak against it. The first is that the 'compromise' of allowing mass sterilization rather than murdering the *Mischlinge* had an established pedigree of which Stuckart will have been well aware.[6] In October 1941 Dr Adolf Pokorny had proposed to Himmler that Soviet POWs might be sterilized, thus making it 'safe' to deploy them as workers on German soil.[7] In the same month the chief of the Reich Chancellery, Lammers, and the chief of the Party's Race-Political Office, Gross, had held a conversation about the *Mischlinge*. Lammers had said he would support the sterilization of all first-degree *Mischlinge* (originally proposed by Eduard Wagner in 1935).[8] The second, even stronger, argument against such a generous interpretation of Stuckart's conduct is his radical approach to mixed marriages. *That* proposal was never going to be postponed on feasibility grounds.

Whatever Stuckart's motives, the RSHA was certainly delighted. At several points in his Jerusalem testimony, Eichmann returned almost with glee to the 'conversion' of Staatssekretär Stuckart. Questioned by his defence lawyer about the atmosphere among the participants, Eichmann said that

Not only did everybody willingly indicate agreement, but there was something else, entirely unexpected, when they outdid and outbid each other, as regards the demand for a Final Solution to the Jewish Question. The biggest surprise, as far as I remember, was not only Bühler, but above all Stuckart, who was always cautious and hesitant, but who suddenly behaved there with unaccustomed enthusiasm.[9]

Cross-examined by the judge about how openly murder had been spoken about at Wannsee, Eichmann said:

Today, I no longer have any detailed recollection of this matter, Your Honour, but I know that these gentlemen stood together and sat together, and in very blunt words they referred to the matter, without putting it down in writing. I would definitely not be able to remember this, if I did not know that at that time I said to myself: Look at that . . . Stuckart, who was always considered to be a very precise and very particular stickler for the law, and here the whole tone and all the manner of speech were totally out of keeping with legal language. That is the only thing, I would say, which has actually remained imprinted on my mind.[10]

Heydrich's behaviour at the end of the conference amply revealed his own satisfaction. In one of a series of interviews given in Argentina before his capture, Eichmann said:

I remember that at the end of this Wannsee Conference Heydrich, Müller and my humble self settled down comfortably by the fireplace and that then for the first time I saw Heydrich smoke a cigar or a cigarette, and I was thinking: today Heydrich is smoking, something I have not seen before. And he drinks cognac – since I had not seen Heydrich take any alcoholic drink in years . . . And after this Wannsee Conference we were sitting together peacefully, and not in order to talk shop, but in order to relax after the long hours of strain. I cannot say any more about this.[11]

In Jerusalem Eichmann reaffirmed that Heydrich's 'satisfaction was quite obvious'[12] and that, despite his own insignificance, as he tried to claim, he had been asked to stay behind for 'a glass or two or three of cognac'.[13]

In some senses, Heydrich's pleasure was probably justified. Wannsee had underlined the RSHA's claim to mastery in the Jewish question. The Ministry of the Interior increasingly subordinated itself to Himmler's leadership even before Himmler himself was appointed minister – and Stuckart became his Staatssekretär. But if Heydrich really believed that he had carried the day on the *Mischling* question, he was soon to be disappointed. It seems, even from the Protocol itself, that he may have broached the issue quite tentatively since his remarks on the *Mischlinge* are described as 'theoretical'.[14] A note from the Ministry for the Eastern Territories' racial expert, Erhard Wetzel, suggested that the whole discussion had been only exploratory: '20th of the 1st, Staatssekretär-Besprechung: Mischlinge of the 1st Degree *no* worse than hitherto. Question merely raised for discussion. General rejection also Führer Chancellery.'[15]

True, there were early signs that Wannsee had indeed changed the climate when, on 29 January, a meeting held in the Ministry for the Eastern Territories decided to treat Soviet *Mischlinge* as Jews.[16] But since these *Mischlinge* were half-Russian (or half-Lithuanian, etc.) rather than half-German, the defensive arguments of the Ministry of the Interior would scarcely have applied anyway. There was little evidence that half-Jews had hitherto enjoyed much protection in Russia. Himmler rejected any formal guidelines on the matter outside Germany: 'We only tie our hands with all these stupid definitions.'[17] So the decision was rather an academic one.

More serious were two follow-up meetings to Wannsee that took place in March and in October 1942, involving subordinates of the Wannsee participants.[18] At both meetings Eichmann and the Party radicals sought to get agreement for Stuckart's compromise proposals at the very least, but if possible to go further and return to Heydrich's suggestions. However, although the meetings passed radical suggestions up the line, on neither occasion did these come to anything. For on thing, mass sterilization did turn out to be impracticable, despite some suggestions in summer 1942 that X-ray treatment might be speedy and effective. For another, both the Justice Ministry and the Ministry of Propaganda were worried about the implications of compulsory divorce. The former was worried about loss of jurisdiction, the latter about the implications on Catholic morale if blanket condemnation issued from the Vatican.[19] The Reich Chancellery also helped to slow down the proposals; decisive, however, was Hitler's unwillingness to tackle the matter in wartime.[20] Lammers said at Nuremberg that, after obtaining a lukewarm response from Hitler in March on the issue of the *Mischlinge*, the gentlemen in the Reich Chancellery interpreted this moment as a definite victory over the RSHA. In October 1943 Justice Minister Otto Georg Thierack and Himmler agreed not to deport *Mischlinge* for the duration of the war.[21]

As far as mixed marriages were concerned, the October 1942 follow-up meeting did reaffirm the commitment to compulsory divorce of Jews. However, here again, the initiative was blocked at a higher level, with Lammers interpreting Hitler's signals as meaning he did not wish to be bothered with such a proposal during the war.[22] Following a decree from Müller in December 1943, the regime did begin to deport formerly privileged Jewish widows after the death of the spouse. Starting in January 1945, some Jewish partners in existing marriages were also deported.[23] For the most part, however, the Jews in privileged mixed marriages were saved. Wannsee had thus failed to provide the decisive breakthrough Heydrich may have hoped for. Ultimately, the axiom had once again proved true that where Hitler was hesitant, policy stagnated.

In relation to 'full' and non-German Jews, there was no such hesitancy. Nineteen forty-two was the most astounding year of murder in the Holocaust, one of the most astounding years of murder in the whole history of mankind. Up to March 1942, less than 10 per cent of the eventual total of the Holocaust's Jewish victims had died, predominantly in the Soviet Union and also some tens of thousands in Chelmno.[24] It was the Soviet POW victims of German neglect, not Jews, whose deaths could be added up in millions. But the period from the beginning of killings at Bełżec in mid-March 1942 through to mid-February 1943 saw the extermination of over half of all the Jews who would die at the Nazis' hands.[25] How significant was the Wannsee conference itself in unleashing this unbelievable tide?

Both Heydrich and Eichmann certainly talked up the meeting's significance at the time. Five days after Wannsee Heydrich sent out a circular to all the regional security police chiefs, attaching Göring's mandate and assuring them that the preparatory measures were now being implemented.[26] Towards the end of February Heydrich sent out copies of the Protocol to the participants, with an accompanying note affirming that 'happily the basic line' had now been 'established as regards the practical execution of the Final Solution of the Jewish question'.[27] In the aftermath of the conference, Eichmann spread the word among his subordinates about the plan to murder Europe's Jews, as Dieter Wisliceny and Hermann Krumey later testified.[28]

In Jerusalem, too, Eichmann continued to underline Wannsee's significance:

... well it is quite easy to verify it, the Conference of Wannsee was very important, for here Heydrich received his authority as the person in charge of the solution, or the final solution of the Jewish question. From this point he regarded himself as having the authority in all these matters.[29]

The outcome of the conference galvanized them both to new efforts. On 31 January 1942 Eichmann sent a circular to all the regional Gestapo centres concerning the new deportation programme. At his trial Eichmann regarded this circular as the first direct consequence of the Wannsee meeting. This confirms that, at the very least, Wannsee opened the way to a massive new wave of deportation, as soon as the transport situation permitted.[30] The circular announced that until then deportations had been constrained by the limited absorption facilities in the east, but that new possibilities of absorbing them were being worked out.[31] This was doubtless a coded reference to mass murder. Transport difficulties prevented the onset of new deportations until March, when Eichmann was again very active, holding a series of meetings, with Jewish advisers posted abroad, with the junior officials from the Wannsee departments on sterilization, and with regional Gestapo leaders, making sure that they stuck to the Wannsee guidelines and did not 'evacuate' elderly Jews who were supposed to go to Theresienstadt.[32]

There are signs, too, that the Protocol spread waves through German officialdom in Europe. Thirty copies were produced; at a cautious estimate each one reached five to ten officials.[33] We know that the officials in Minsk soon heard about it, while on 23 March the Jewish expert in the German embassy in Paris, Carltheo Zeitschel, wrote to his superiors in the Foreign Office, saying he had heard that a Staatssekretäre meeting had taken place and asking for a copy of the minutes.[34]

At the Wannsee conference Heydrich made clear that he had yet to produce the overall plan required of him by Göring. Whether he ever submitted it, we do not know. It has been argued that Goebbels refers to such a document in his diary entry from 7 March, 'I am reading a detailed paper from the SD and Police on the Final Solution of the Jewish Question. It raises a large number of issues. The Jewish Question must be solved now on a pan-European scale.'[35] However, Heydrich's note accompanying the Protocol made clear that any final report could be completed only once the follow-up meeting to Wannsee (on 6 March) had taken place.[36] Between the holding of that meeting on 6 March and Goebbels's entry on the 7th there was no time for the production and dissemination of such a comprehensive document. It seems more likely, therefore, that Goebbels was referring to the Wannsee Protocol itself (which he will have received at the beginning of March), and that it became the surrogate document of 'closure'.[37] The Protocol was probably the closest the Nazis ever came to writing down their overall plan of genocide.

In the Generalgouvernement, it was only in late January that preparations for the deportation of Lublin Jews to Bełżec gathered momentum.[38] Around this time Himmler and HSSPF Krüger carried out personal changes among the SSPF in the Generalgouvernement. Only the really radical figures – Globocnik and Katzmann – remained in post. Those who did not seem radical enough were replaced.[39] In White Russia it was only from mid-February that the surviving German Jews languishing there were murdered.[40] February 1942 also saw a significant expansion of plans for crematoria and gas chambers at Auschwitz. In March a new wave of deportations of German Jews began – this time to the Lublin area of Poland. At the same time Slovakian Jews started to be dispatched to Auschwitz, where they would be worked to death rather than gassed. Lublin Jews were first murdered in Bełżec in large numbers in the same month, while Sobibor would claim its first victims in April.[41]

This dismal narrative does not necessarily establish Wannsee itself as the decisive catalyst. For one thing, as we know, the killings at Bełżec had been in the planning since the previous October. Auschwitz, too, had been set to come into operation since test killings the previous autumn. Transports would presumably have resumed without Wannsee. For another, historians such as Peter Longerich would point out that German Jews sent in March 1942 to Piaski, Izbica and Zamosc as well as to Warsaw were, like their predecessors in 1941, not killed straight away, but instead packed into the hovels of Polish Jews who were sent on to the gas chambers. Longerich argues that as late as March 1942 the killings at Bełżec still conformed to the 'old' pattern of piecemeal 'clearing operations' to make way for deportations. He argues that the pattern was broken only in the period May–July 1942, which saw a massive expansion in the killing programme. Some further decision must have been taken, Longerich argues, before the Nazi killings became truly comprehensive.[42]

Part of the problem here lies in what we define as a 'decision'. Himmler's direct and repeated involvement in widening the scope of killings in 1942 is well documented. The beginnings of mass murder through poison gas in the Generalgouvernement coincided with Himmler's visit to Krakow and Lublin on 13 and 14 March 1942. On 17 April 1942, after consultations with Hitler the preceding day, Himmler personally ordered the killing of the western European Jews in Łódź. His visit to Warsaw on that day was also accompanied by a decision to construct a new extermination camp, Treblinka. Heydrich's death in early June, in the wake of an assassination attempt, served only to emphasize Himmler's leadership role and to add extra ferocity to his campaign. Following meetings with Hitler on 14 July, Himmler launched a new, still more intense, wave of killing. On 18 July he was in Auschwitz to inaugurate the real phase of mass gassings there. He was in Lublin the following day, from where he dispatched a telegram to HSSPF Krüger, ordering that, with a few exceptions, all Jews in the Generalgouvernement should be killed by the end of the year. Three days later, on 22 July, the most intense phase of the Final Solution began with the deportations from Warsaw to Treblinka. In relation to the extermination of the last Jewish communities in the Reichskommissariat Ukraine, which began in May–June 1942, we have one of the few written orders for murder from Himmler. To that extent, even after Wannsee, the process demonstrably did not function on its own, and involved Himmler's continual interventions – on several occasions, it seems, after consultation with Hitler.[43]

In Jerusalem Eichmann, too, sought to refute the prosecutor's suggestion that after Wannsee the operation ran like clockwork:

ACCUSED [Eichmann]: That is wrong, Mr Attorney General. Each individual wave had to be ordered afresh. The documents show this also. And once such orders had been issued, if I was competent to act and received orders from my superior, the entire matter of trains, for example, also had to be dealt with. That is correct. As for the camps in the East, or the absorption stations, they were named – how they . . .

PRESIDING JUDGE: The question is directed to the physical possibilities of extermination – that is how I understand the question, and what would appear to depend on two factors – as mentioned by the Attorney General – transport possibilities and absorption possibilities. Is that correct?

ACCUSED: In principle that is correct, Your Honour, but first the orders had to be issued.

ATTORNEY GENERAL: But an order already existed – there was this order – this order by the Führer from summer of 1941,[44] and you saw this document signed by Goering.

ACCUSED: In that case for all practical purposes, after the Wannsee Conference Heydrich, for example, would have had to say to me: 'Well, Eichmann, everything is settled, approved, see to it now, do what you want, but the matter must be settled one-two-three.'

But that is not how things were: Himmler kept issuing orders, time and time again he issued orders. All the many hundreds of offices who were somehow involved had to carry out their part, and I was also unfortunately caught up in this. As a result of these measures I had to deal with the matters on which I received orders – I have never denied this and am not denying it, either. I cannot deny it, because that is what happened . . .[45]

This was not just Eichmann hiding behind orders; Himmler really had been continually involved. And yet developments in 1942 show an obvious difference from the situation in autumn 1941. In September and October 1941 transports were dispatched without a clear idea of what would happen to them, and to areas where there was no definite policy of what was to happen. Regional officials felt their way and did some of the centre's thinking for it, though always in close liaison with Berlin. Once transports resumed in March 1942 this was no longer the case. No one was sent to a region where the ultimate fate was unclear. German Jews were sent to the Lublin region where extermination camps were in place, and where there was a clear expectation that first the Poles and then they would be murdered. There was no indeterminate eastern territory being considered. Above all, though, the whole operation was now being planned from Berlin.

That does not mean that decisions did not still need to be taken. Throughout 1942, for example, there would be a fluctuating balance of sorts drawn between manpower needs and the project of genocide. Given the fact that Germany would lose the war and thus be unable to complete their programme, Himmler's interventions and the shifting pressures for or against retaining Jewish manpower were to be of vital significance in deciding what remnant of European Jewry might survive. But they were not decisions about whether to kill or not, simply about when and in what order to kill. In this respect, the Wannsee Protocol really did capture a decisive transition in German policy, a transition from quasi-genocidal deportations to a clear programme of murder.

Wannsee itself was not the moment of decision. Nobody at Wannsee, not even Heydrich, was senior enough to decide on such matters. The fate of the *Mischlinge* revealed that, if the right arguments could be passed up to Hitler, agreements secured at the Wannsee conference could be undone. Conversely, where Hitler's approval was assured, Himmler would undoubtedly have proceeded even if Heydrich had not secured the active and passive assents he obtained at Wannsee. The Wannsee Protocol was rather a signpost indicating that genocide had become official policy. Yet Heydrich undoubtedly took the assent he had engineered at Wannsee very seriously. The signals he and Eichmann gave out after the event showed it had immeasurably strengthened their confidence. Even in May, visiting security officials in France for the last time before his assassination, Heydrich's account of the planning for the Final Solution emphasized the agreements reached on 20 January.[46] Speaking to one another with great politeness, sipping their cognac, the Staatssekretäre really had cleared the way for genocide.

Appendix A: Translation of the Protocol[1]

Stamp: Top Secret

30 copies

16th copy

Minutes of discussion

I. The following persons took part in the discussion about the final solution of the Jewish question which took place in Berlin, Am Großen Wannsee No. 56/58 on 20 January 1942.

Gauleiter Dr Meyer and Reichsamtleiter Dr Leibbrandt, Reich Ministry for the Occupied Eastern Territories

Staatssekretär Dr Stuckart, Reich Ministry for the Interior

Staatssekretär Neumann, Plenipotentiary for the Four-Year Plan

Staatssekretär Dr Freisler, Reich Ministry of Justice

Staatssekretär Dr Bühler, Office of the Generalgouvernement

Unterstaatssekretär Dr Luther, Foreign Office

SS-Oberführer Klopfer, Party Chancellery

Ministerialdirektor Kritzinger, Reich Chancellery

SS-Gruppenführer Hofmann, Race and Settlement Main Office

SS-Gruppenführer Müller

SS-Obersturmbannführer Eichmann, Reich Main Security Office

SS-Oberführer Dr Schöngarth, Chief of the Security Police and the SD in the Generalgouvernement – Security Police and SD

SS-Sturmbannführer Dr Lange, Commander of the Security Police and the SD for the General District Latvia, as deputy of the Chief of the Security Police and the SD for the Reich Commissariat 'Ostland' – Security Police and SD

II. At the beginning of the discussion Chief of the Security Police and of the SD, SS-Obergruppenführer Heydrich, reported that the Reich Marshal had delegated to him the preparations for the Final Solution of the Jewish question in Europe and that this discussion had been called for the purpose of clarifying fundamental questions. The wish of the Reich Marshal to have a draft sent to him concerning organizational, policy and technical prerequisites for the Final Solution of the European Jewish question makes it necessary to ensure in advance that the central organizations involved be brought together and their policies properly coordinated.

Overall control of the Final Solution of the Jewish question lies, irrespective of geographical boundaries, with the Reichsführer SS and Chief of the German Police (Chief of the Security Police and SD).

The Chief of the Security Police and SD then gave a short report of the struggle which had been carried on thus far against this enemy, the essential points being the following:

a) the expulsion of the Jews from every sphere of life of the German people,

b) the expulsion of the Jews from the living space of the German people.

In pursuit of these ends, the only provisional solution available had been a planned acceleration of Jewish emigration out of Reich terriroty.

By order of the Reich Marshal, a Reich Central Office for Jewish Emigration was created in January 1939, under the leadership of the Chief of the Security Police and SD. Its most important tasks were

a) to make all necessary arrangements for the preparation for an increased emigration of the Jews,

b) to direct the flow of emigration,

c) to speed the procedure of emigration in each individual case.

The aim of all this was to cleanse German living space of Jews in a legal manner. The drawbacks of such enforced accelerated emigration were clear to all involved. In the absence of any alternative, however, these drawbacks had initially to be accepted.

In the ensuing period, the tasks associated with emigration became not just a German problem, but one confronting the authorities of the countries to which the flow of emigrants was directed. Financial difficulties, such as the demand by various foreign governments for increasing sums of money to be presented at the time of the landing, the lack of shipping space, increasing restriction of entry permits, or the cancelling of such, radically augmented the difficulties of emigration. In spite of these difficulties, 537,000 Jews were sent out of the country between the takeover of power and the deadline of 31 October 1941. Of these

approximately 360,000 were in Germany proper on 30 January 1933
approximately 147,000 were in Austria (Ostmark) on 15 March 1938
approximately 30,000 were in the Protectorate of Bohemia and Moravia on 15 March 1939.

The Jews themselves, or their political organizations, financed the emigration. In order to avoid impoverished Jews remaining behind, the principle was followed that wealthy Jews have to finance the emigration of poor Jews; this was arranged by imposing a suitable tax, i.e. an emigration tax, which was used for financial arrangements in connection with the emigration of poor Jews and was imposed according to wealth.

Apart from the necessary Reichsmark exchange, foreign currency had to be presented at the time of landing. In order to prevent a drain of German foreign exchange holdings, the foreign Jewish financial organizations were – with the help of Jewish organizations in Germany – made responsible for arranging an adequate amount of foreign currency. Up to 30 October 1941 these foreign Jews donated a total of around 9,500,000 dollars.

In the meantime the Reichsführer SS and Chief of the German

Police had prohibited emigration of Jews due to the dangers of an emigration in wartime and due to the possibilities of the east.

III. Instead of emigration, the new solution has emerged, after prior approval by the Führer, of evacuating Jews to the east.

These actions are nevertheless to be seen only as temporary relief but they are providing the practical experience which is of great significance for the coming Final Solution of the Jewish question.

Approximately eleven million Jews will be involved in the Final Solution of the European Jewish question, distributed as follows among the individual countries:

Country	Number
A.	
Germany proper	131,800
Austria	43,700
Eastern territories	420,000
General Government	2,284,000
Bialystok	400,000
Protectorate Bohemia and Moravia	74,200
Estonia	free of Jews
Latvia	3,500
Lithuania	34,000
Belgium	43,000
Denmark	5,600
France / occupied territory	165,000
unoccupied territory	700,000
Greece	69,600
Netherlands	160,800
Norway	1,300
B.	
Bulgaria	48,000

England	330,000
Finland	2,300
Ireland	4,000
Italy including Sardinia	58,000
Albania	200
Croatia	40,000
Portugal	3,000
Romania including Bessarabia	342,000
Sweden	8,000
Switzerland	18,000
Serbia	10,000
Slovakia	88,000
Spain	6,000
Turkey (European portion)	55,500
Hungary	742,800
USSR	5,000,000
Ukraine	2,994,684
White Russia excluding Bialystok	446,484

Total over 11,000,000

The number of Jews given here for foreign countries includes, however, only those Jews who still adhere to the Jewish faith, since some countries still do not have a definition of the term 'Jew' according to racial principles. Dealing with the problem in these individual countries will meet with difficulties due to the attitude and outlook of the people there, especially in Hungary and Romania. Thus, for example, even today the Jew can buy documents in Romania that will officially prove his foreign citizenship.

The influence of the Jews in all walks of life in the USSR is well known. Approximately five million Jews live in the European part of the USSR, in the Asian part scarcely ¼ million.

The breakdown of Jews residing in the European part of the USSR according to trades was approximately as follows:

Agriculture	9.1%
Urban workers	14.8%
In trade	20.0%
Employed by the state	23.4%
In private occupations such as medical profession, press, theatre, etc.	32.7%

In the course of the Final Solution and under appropriate leadership, the Jews should be put to work in the east. In large, single-sex labour columns, Jews fit to work will work their way eastwards constructing roads. Doubtless the large majority will be eliminated by natural causes. Any final remnant that survives will doubtless consist of the most resistant elements. They will have to be dealt with appropriately, because otherwise, by natural selection, they would form the germ cell of a new Jewish revival. (See the experience of history.)

In the course of the practical execution of the Final Solution, Europe will be combed through from west to east. Germany proper, including the Protectorate of Bohemia and Moravia, will have to be dealt with first due to the housing problem and additional social and political necessities.

The evacuated Jews will first be sent, in stages, to so-called transit ghettos, from where they will be transported to the east.

SS-Obergruppenführer Heydrich went on to say that an important prerequisite for the evacuation as such is the exact definition of the persons involved.

It is not intended to evacuate Jews over sixty-five years old, but to send them to an old-age ghetto – Theresienstadt is being considered for this purpose.

In addition to these age groups – of the approximately 280,000 Jews in Germany proper and Austria on 31 October 1941, approximately 30 per cent are over sixty-five years old – severely wounded veterans and Jews with war decorations (Iron Cross I) will be accepted in the old-age ghettos. With this expedient solution, in one fell swoop many interventions will be prevented.

The larger evacuation actions would commence when the military situation allowed. Regarding the handling of the Final Solution in those European countries occupied and influenced by us, it was proposed that the appropriate experts of the Foreign Office discuss the matter with the relevant official of the security police and SD.

In Slovakia and Croatia the matter is no longer so difficult, since the most substantial problems in this respect have already been brought near a solution. In Romania the government has in the meantime also appointed a commissioner for Jewish affairs. In order to settle the question in Hungary, it will soon be necessary to force an adviser for Jewish questions on to the Hungarian government.

With regard to taking up preparations for dealing with the problem in Italy, SS-Obergruppenführer Heydrich considers it opportune to contact the chief of police with a view to these problems.

In occupied and unoccupied France, the registration of Jews for evacuation will in all probability proceed without great difficulty.

Unterstaatssekretär Luther calls attention in this matter to the fact that in some countries, such as the Scandinavian states, difficulties will arise if this problem is dealt with thoroughly and that it will therefore be advisable to defer actions in these countries. In view of the small numbers of Jews affected, this deferral will in any case not cause any substantial limitation.

The Foreign Office sees no great difficulties for southeast and western Europe.

SS-Gruppenführer Hofmann plans to send an expert to Hungary from the Race and Settlement Main Office for general orientation at the time when the Chief of the Security Police and SD takes up the matter there. It was decided to assign this expert from the Race and Settlement Main Office, who will not work actively, as an assistant to the police attaché.

IV. In planning the Final Solution, the Nuremberg Laws will in effect provide the general framework, though a prerequisite for reaching an overall solution is finding an answer to the question of mixed marriages and persons of mixed blood.

The Chief of the Security Police and the SD discusses the following points, at first theoretically, in regard to a letter from the chief of the Reich Chancellery:

1) Treatment of Persons of Mixed Blood of the First Degree
Persons of mixed blood of the first degree will, as regards the Final Solution of the Jewish question, be treated as Jews.
From this treatment the following exceptions will be made:
a) Persons of mixed blood of the first degree married to persons of German blood if their marriage has resulted in children (persons of mixed blood of the second degree). These persons of mixed blood of the second degree are to be treated essentially as Germans.
b) Persons of mixed blood of the first degree, for whom the highest offices of the Party and state have already issued exemption permits in any sphere of life.

Each individual case must be examined, and it is not ruled out that the decision may be made to the detriment of the person of mixed blood.

The prerequisite for any exemption must always be the personal merit of the person of mixed blood (not the merit of the parent or spouse of German blood).

Persons of mixed blood of the first degree who are exempted from evacuation will be sterilized in order to prevent any offspring and to eliminate the problem of persons of mixed blood once and for all. Such sterilization will be voluntary. But it is the precondition for remaining in the Reich. The sterilized 'person of mixed blood' is thereafter free of all restrictions to which he was previously subjected.

2) Treatment of Persons of Mixed Blood of the Second Degree
Persons of mixed blood of the second degree will be treated essentially as persons of German blood, with the exception of the following cases, in which the persons of mixed blood of the second degree will be considered as Jews:
a) The person of mixed blood of the second degree was born of a bastard marriage (both parents persons of mixed blood).
b) The person of mixed blood of the second degree has a racially

especially undesirable appearance that marks him outwardly as a Jew.

c) The person of mixed blood of the second degree has a particularly bad police and political record that shows that he feels and behaves like a Jew.

In these cases, however, exceptions should not be made if the person of mixed blood of the second degree has married a person of German blood.

3) Marriages between Full Jews and Persons of German Blood

Here it must be decided from case to case whether the Jewish partner should be evacuated or, in view of the effects of such a step on the German relatives of the marriage, sent to an old-age ghetto.

4) Marriages between Persons of Mixed Blood of the First Degree and Persons of German Blood

a) Without Children

If no children have resulted from the marriage, the person of mixed blood of the first degree will be evacuated or sent to an old-age ghetto (same treatment as in the case of marriages between full Jews and persons of German blood, point 3).

b) With Children

If children have resulted from the marriage (persons of mixed blood of the second degree), they will, if they are to be treated as Jews, be evacuated or sent to a ghetto along with the parent of mixed blood of the first degree. If these children are to be treated as Germans (regular cases), they are exempted from evacuation as is therefore the parent of mixed blood of the first degree.

5) Marriages between Persons of Mixed Blood of the First Degree and Persons of Mixed Blood of the First Degree or Jews

In these marriages all members of the family (including the children) will be treated as Jews and therefore be evacuated or sent to an old-age ghetto.

6) Marriages between Persons of Mixed Blood of the First Degree and Persons of Mixed Blood of the Second Degree

In these marriages both partners will be evacuated or sent to an old-age ghetto without consideration of whether the marriage has produced children, since possible children will as a rule have stronger Jewish blood than the Jewish person of mixed blood of the second degree.

SS-Gruppenführer Hofmann is of the view that extensive use should be made of sterilization; particularly as the *Mischling*, presented with the choice of evacuation, would rather submit to sterilization.

State Secretary Dr Stuckart points out that the practical implementation of the strategies outlined for dealing with the mixed-race and mixed-marriage questions will entail endless administrative work. In order, on the other hand, to ensure the biological facts are fully taken on board, State Secretary Dr Stuckart proposes proceeding to forced sterilization.

Furthermore, to simplify the problem of mixed marriages, possibilities must be considered, such that the law in effect says: 'These marriages have been dissolved.'

With regard to the question of the effect of the evacuation of Jews on the economy, State Secretary Neumann stated that as long as replacements were not available, Jews employed in industries vital to the war effort could not be evacuated.

SS-Obergruppenführer Heydrich pointed out according to the rules he had approved for carrying out the evacuations these Jews would not be evacuated anyway.

State Secretary Dr Bühler stated that the Generalgouvernement would welcome it if the Final Solution of this problem could begin in the Generalgouvernement, since on the one hand transportation does not play such a large role there nor would the question of labour supply hamper this action. The Jews must be removed from the territory of the Generalgouvernement as quickly as possible because of the particular danger there of epidemics being brought on by Jews. Jewish black-market activities were persistently destabilizing the region's economy. The 2½ million Jews in the region were in any case largely unable to work.

State Secretary Dr Bühler stated further that the solution to the

Jewish question in the Generalgouvernement is the responsibility of the Chief of the Security Police and SD and that his efforts would be supported by the officials of the Generalgouvernement. He had only one request – that the Jewish question be solved as quickly as possible.

In conclusion the various possible kinds of solution were discussed, with both Gauleiter Dr Meyer and State Secretary Dr Bühler taking the position that certain preparatory activities for the Final Solution should be carried out immediately in the territories in question, without alarming the populace.

With a final request from the Chief of the Security Police and SD that the participants provide him with necessary cooperation and assistance in carrying out his tasks, the meeting was closed.

Notes

1. 'Perhaps the most shameful document'

1 The international war crimes trials ended in 1946. The US then prosecuted second-rank officials in subsequent trials, also at Nuremberg. The 'Ministries Case' involved the civil servants at Wannsee (among others). See *Trials of War Criminals Before the Nuremberg Military Tribunals Under Control Council Law No. 10*, Volumes 13–15: *'The Ministries Case'*, (Nuremberg, October 1946–April 1949).

2 My translation from Robert M. W. Kempner, *Ankläger einer Epoche. Lebenserinnerungen* (Ullstein; Frankfurt am Main, Berlin, Vienna, 1983), pp. 310–11, here p. 311. Brigadier General Telford Taylor had replaced Robert Jackson as chief US prosecutor.

3 John A. S. Grenville, 'Die "Endlösung" and die "Judenmischlinge" im Dritten Reich', in Ursula Büttner with Werner Johe and Angelika Voss (eds.), *Das Unrechtsregime: Internationale Forschung über den Nationalsozialismus* (Christians Verlag; Hamburg, 1986), pp. 91–121, here p. 108.

4 Kempner, *Ankläger*, pp. 310–12.

5 Leni Yahil, 'Himmler's Timetable', *Yad Vashem Studies* 28 (2000), pp. 351–62, here p. 352.

6 Eberhard Jäckel, 'On the Purpose of the Wannsee Conference', in James S. Pacy and Alan P. Wertheimer (eds.), *Perspectives on the Holocaust. Essays in Honor of Raul Hilberg* (Westview Press; Boulder, San Francisco, Oxford, 1995), pp. 39–50, here p. 39.

7 On the Protocol's authenticity, Wolfgang Scheffler, 'Die Wannsee-Konferenz und Ihre Historische Bedeutung', in the brochure edited by Gedenkstätte Haus der Wannsee-Konferenz, 'Erinnern für die Zukunft'

(printed by the Gedenkstätte, Berlin, no date [1992]), pp. 17-34, here pp. 30-31. 8 The best summary is Eberhard Jäckel and Jürgen Rohwer, *Der Mord an den Juden im Zweiten Weltkrieg* (Deutsche Verlags-Anstalt; Stuttgart, 1985).

9 Surveys of these debates usually list the same few names – Lucy Davidowicz and Gerald Fleming, on the one hand, Martin Broszat and Hans Mommsen on the other – precisely because the vast majority of historians pursued judicious syntheses.

10 For the clearest and most carefully argued syntheses on these lines see Christopher R. Browning, *Fateful Months: Essays on the Emergence of the Final Solution* (Holmes and Meier; New York, 1985); Christopher R. Browning, *The Path to Genocide. Essays on Launching the Final Solution* (Cambridge University Press; Cambridge, 1992); Philippe Burrin, *Hitler and the Jews. The Genesis of the Holocaust* (Edward Arnold; London, 1994).

11 See Raul Hilberg, *The Destruction of the European Jews* (revised and definitive edition), (Holmes and Meier; New York and London, 1985).

12 Hans Mommsen, 'The Realization of the Unthinkable: The "Final Solution of the Jewish Question" in the Third Reich', in Hans Mommsen, *From Weimar to Auschwitz. Essays in German History* (Basil Blackwell; Oxford, 1991), pp. 224-53; Martin Broszat, 'Hitler und die "Endlösung". Aus Anlaß der Thesen von David Irving', *Vierteljahrshefte für Zeitgeschichte*, vol. 25 (1977), 4, pp. 739-75.

13 Daniel Goldhagen was seeking to explain the motivation of perpetrators at the lower level. See his *Hitler's Willing Executioners. Ordinary Germans and the Holocaust* (Abacus edition; London, 1997).

14 Saul Friedländer, *Nazi Germany and the Jews. The Years of Persecution 1933-1939* (Phoenix Giant; London, 1997) and Ian Kershaw, *Hitler 1936-1945. Vol. 2, Nemesis* (Allen Lane The Penguin Press; Harmondsworth, 2000).

15 Ulrich Herbert, *Best. Biographische Studien über Radikalismus, Weltanschauung und Vernunft, 1903-1989* (J. H. W. Dietz Verlag; Bonn, 1996); Peter Longerich, *Politik der Vernichtung. Eine Gesamtdarstellung der Nationalsozialistischen Judenverfolgung* (Piper Verlag; Munich and Zürich, 1998).

16 Some of the best of this recent work is summarized in Ulrich Herbert (ed.), *National Socialist Extermination Policy* (Berghahn Books; Oxford and New York, 1999).

2. *Mein Kampf* to mass murder

1 Philippe Burrin, *Hitler and the Jews. The Genesis of the Holocaust* (Edward Arnold; London, 1994), p. 26, citing Hitler in a conversation in 1923.

2 Hitler's comments in the Leipzig newspaper *Der Nationalsozialist* reproduced in Eberhard Jäckel, *Hitler's World View. A Blueprint for Power* (Harvard University Press; Cambridge, Mass. and London, 1981), p. 57.

3 Jäckel, *Hitler's World View*, p. 58.

4 Cited in John Lukacs, *The Hitler of History* (Vintage Books; New York, 1997), p. 182.

5 Richard J. Evans, *Lying About Hitler. History, Holocaust and the David Irving Trial* (Basic Books; New York, 2001), pp. 72-3.

6 Max Domarus (ed.), *Hitler, Speeches and Proclamations 1932-1945.* Vol. 2, *1935-1938* (I. B. Tauris; London, 1992), p. 758.

7 Oded Heilbronner, 'The Place of Anti-Semitism in Modern German History', *Leo Baeck Institute Year Book* 20 (1990), p. 571.

8 Cited in Hermann Graml, 'Zur Genesis der Endlösung', in Ursula Büttner (ed.), *Das Unrechtsregime. Internationale Forschung über den Nationalsozialismus. Band 2: Verfolgung - Exil - Belasteter Neubeginn* (Christians Verlag; Hamburg, 1986), pp. 2-18.

9 H. G. Adler, *Der Verwaltete Mensch. Studien zur Deportation der Juden aus Deutschland* (J. C. B. Mohr (Paul Siebeck); Tübingen, 1974), pp. xxv-xxvi.

10 Burrin, *Hitler and the Jews*, p. 30.

11 Hitler in a letter to Adolf Gemlich. Cited in Saul Friedländer, *Nazi Germany and the Jews. The Years of Persecution 1933-1939* (Phoenix Giant; London, 1997), p. 72.

12 Peter Longerich, *Politik der Vernichtung. Eine Gesamtdarstellung der Nationalsozialistischen Judenverfolgung* (Piper Verlag; Munich and Zürich, 1998).

13 Hans Mommsen, 'The Realization of the Unthinkable: The "Final Solution of the Jewish Question" in the Third Reich', in Hans Mommsen, *From Weimar to Auschwitz. Essays in German History* (Basil Blackwell; Oxford 1991), pp. 224-53, here p. 230.

14 Günther Deschner, *Reinhard Heydrich. Statthalter der Totalen Macht. Biographie* (Bechtle Verlag; Esslingen am Neckar, 1977), p. 184.

15 The reference here is to the classic: Karl A. Schleunes, *The Twisted Road to Auschwitz. Nazi Policy Towards German Jews 1933–1939* (Urbana; Illinois, 1970).

16 Mommsen, 'Realization', p. 227.

17 A view encouraged by Bernhard Lösener, 'Dokumentation. Das Reichsministerium des Innern und die Judengesetzgebung', in *Vierteljahrshefte für Zeitgeschichte*, vol. 19 (1961), pp. 262–312.

18 Mommsen, 'Realization', p. 233; Uwe Dietrich Adam, *Judenpolitik im Dritten Reich* (Droste Verlag; Düsseldorf, 1971), pp. 206–7.

19 Friedländer, *Nazi Germany and the Jews*, pp. 146–7.

20 See below, p. 80.

21 Cited in Ian Kershaw, *Hitler, 1936–1945*. Vol. 2, *Nemesis* (Allen Lane The Penguin Press; Harmondsworth, 2000), p. 1.

22 Friedländer, *Nazi Germany and the Jews*, p. 181.

23 See the discussion in Evans, *Lying About Hitler*, pp. 52–62..

24 Cited in Richard Breitman, *The Architect of Genocide. Himmler and the Final Solution* (Alfred A. Knopf; New York, 1991), p. 54.

25 Raul Hilberg, *Perpetrators, Victims, Bystanders. The Jewish Catastrophe 1933–1945* (HarperCollins; London, 1992), pp. 21–4.

26 Michael Wildt (ed.), *Die Judenpolitik des SD 1935 bis 1938. Eine Dokumentation* (R. Oldenbourg Verlag; Munich, 1995), pp. 40–45, 100–105; Claudia Steur, *Theodor Dannecker. Ein Funktionär der 'Endlösung'* (Klartext Verlag; Essen, 1997), p. 25; Longerich, *Politik der Vernichtung*, p. 210; Deschner, *Heydrich*, p. 166.

27 See Detlev Grieswelle, 'Hitlers Rhetorik in der Weimarer Zeit' (Diss; Saarbrück, 1969); Friedländer, *Nazi Germany and the Jews*, p. 102.

28 Longerich, *Politik der Vernichtung*, pp. 25–30.

29 Cited in Hans-Heinrich Wilhelm, *Die Einsatzgruppe A der Sicherheitspolizei und des SD 1941/1942*, (Peter Lang; Frankfurt am Main, 1996), pp. 15–16, n 9.

30 See Bernd Weisbrod, 'The Crisis of Bourgeois Society in Interwar Germany', in Richard Bessel (ed.), *Fascist Italy and Nazi Germany. Comparisons and Contrasts* (Cambridge University Press; Cambridge, 1996), pp. 23–39, here p. 36 and Bernd Weisbrod, 'Violence and Sacrifice: Imagining the Nation in Weimar Germany', in Hans Mommsen (ed.), *The Third Reich Between Vision and Reality. New Perspectives on German History 1918–1945* (Berg; Oxford, 2001), pp. 5–21.

31 Ulrich Herbert, 'Vernichtungspolitik. Neue Antworten und Fragen zur Geschichte des "Holocaust"', in Herbert (ed.), *Nationalsozialistische Vernichtungspolitik*, pp. 9–66, here p. 41.

32 Ulrich Herbert, *Best. Biographische Studien über Radikalismus, Weltanschauung und Vernunft, 1903–1989* (J. H. W. Dietz Verlag; Bonn, 1996), pp. 42–68.

33 Ulrich Herbert, 'Ideological Legitimization and Political Practice of the Leadership of the National Socialist Secret Police', in Mommsen, *The Third Reich Between Vision and Reality*, pp. 95–108.

34 Herbert, 'Ideological Legitimization', p. 95; Deschner, *Heydrich*, p. 83.

35 Heydrich's biographer Deschner himself falls prey to this self-image.

36 Herbert, *Best*, pp. 88–100.

37 See the remarks about Dannecker's background in Steur, *Dannecker*; see also Deschner, *Heydrich*, pp. 160, 166.

38 Michael Burleigh, *The Third Reich. A New History* (Macmillan; London, 2000), p. 189.

39 Adler, *Verwaltete Mensch*, p. 3.

40 Christopher Browning, *The Final Solution and the German Foreign Office. A Study of Referat DIII of Abteilung Deutschland 1940–1943* (New York; Holmes and Meier, 1978), pp. 12–17. Wildt (ed.), *Die Judenpolitik des SD*, pp. 40–5, 100–105.

41 Avraham Barkai, *From Boycott to Annihilation. The Economic Struggle of German Jews, 1933–1943*, (University Press of New England; Hanover, 1989).

42 Graml, 'Zur Genesis der Endlösung', p. 6.

43 Burrin, *Hitler and the Jews*, p. 60.

44 Helmut Krausnick and Hans-Heinrich Wilhelm, *Die Truppe des Weltanschauungskrieges: Die Einsatzgruppen der Sicherheitspolizei und des SD, 1938–1942* (Deutsche Verlags-Anstalt; Stuttgart, 1981), p. 623.

45 *Judenkenner*, 27.10.1935, cited in Adler, *Verwaltete Mensch*, p. 60.

46 Cited in Burrin, *Hitler and the Jews*, p. 62.

47 Mommsen, 'Realization', p. 233.

48 Henry Friedlander, *The Origins of Nazi Genocide. From Euthanasia to the Final Solution* (University of North Carolina Press; Chapel Hill and London, 1995), p. 39.

49 Friedländer, *Nazi Germany and the Jews*, p. 312. See also the Heydrich speech in Breitman, *Architect*, p. 59.

50 Hitler was taken by surprise that the Polish issue should have led to European war and even in early September, he was prepared to negotiate on terms with the Poles. Martin Broszat, *Nationalsozialistische Polenpolitik 1939–1945* (Deutsche Verlags-Anstalt; Stuttgart, 1961), p. 10.

51 Tens of thousands of Jews were driven under the greatest brutality across the demarcation line with the Soviet Union, sometimes only to find themselves forced back by the Soviets. An agreement with the USSR put a stop to these measures in December 1939. On the evidence that the intentions at this stage were not genocidal, see Krausnick and Wilhelm, *Truppe*, pp. 71, 107; Hans Safrian, *Die Eichmann-Männer* (Europa Verlag; Vienna, Zürich, 1993), pp. 71–2.

52 Safrian, *Eichmann-Männer*, pp. 72ff; Dieter Pohl, *Von der 'Judenpolitik' zum Judenmord. Der Distrikt Lublin des Generalgouvernements 1939–1944* (Peter Lang; Frankfurt am Main, Berlin, 1993), pp. 54–5.

53 Ralf Ogorreck, *Die Einsatzgruppen und die 'Genesis der Endlösung'*, (Metropol Verlag; Berlin, 1996), p. 172.

54 Burrin, *Hitler and the Jews*, p. 77; Adler, *Verwaltete Mensch*, p. 72.

55 The historian Richard Breitman has been among the most distinguished of those who believe that Hitler and Himmler were in fact committed to genocide from the beginning of 1941. See the discussion below, p. 36. There is no room here to respond to all the arguments, but see the account in Longerich, *Politik der Vernichtung*, pp. 273–92.

56 Safrian, *Eichmann-Männer*, p. 88.

57 Pohl, *Von der Judenpolitik*, pp. 54–5.

58 Safrian, *Eichmann-Männer*, pp. 68, 79ff, 90.

59 Longerich, *Politik der Vernichtung*, p. 243.

60 Jürgen Förster, 'The Relation Between Operation Barbarossa as an Ideological War of Extermination and the Final Solution', in David Cesarani (ed.), *The Final Solution. Origins and Implementation* (Routledge; London, 1994, pp. 85–102), here p. 87; Dieter Pohl, 'Die Ermordung der Juden im Generalgouvernement', in Ulrich Herbert (ed.), *Nationalsozialistische Vernichtungspolitik 1939–1945. Neue Forschungen und Kontroversen* (Fischer; Frankfurt am Main, 1998), pp. 98–121, here p. 99.

61 Friedlander, *Origins*, pp. 62, 86ff, 136–7, 272; Götz Aly, ' "Judenumsiedlung". Überlegungen zur Politischen Vorgeschichte des Holocaust', in Ulrich Herbert (ed.), *Nationalsozialistische Vernichtungspolitik*, pp. 67–97, here p. 86.

62 Pohl, *Von der Judenpolitik*, pp. 26ff; Krausnick and Wilhelm, *Truppe*, pp. 80–87; Förster, 'Operation Barbarossa and the Final Solution', pp. 88–9.

63 Breitman, *Architect*, p. 139.

64 Susanne Heim and Götz Aly, 'The Holocaust and Population Policy. Remarks on the Decision on the "Final Solution" ', *Yad Vashem Studies* 24, 1994, pp. 45–70, here p. 58.

65 Safrian, *Eichmann-Männer*, p. 79.

66 Ibid., p. 71, 97, 106.

67 Report cited in Jeremy Noakes and Geoffrey Pridham, *Nazism 1919– 1945*, vol. 3, p. 1094.

68 Burrin, *Hitler and the Jews*, p. 95.

69 At various times leading generals Manstein, Guderian, Hoth, Küchler and Reichenau all endorsed the struggle against Jewish subhumans. See Wilhelm, *Einsatzgruppe A*, pp. 15–16, n 9.

70 Reprinted in Yitzhak Arad, Yisrael Gutman and Abraham Margaliot, *Documents on the Holocaust* (University of Nebraska Press; Lincoln and London/ *Yad Vashem*, Jerusalem, Bison Books Edition, 1999), p. 376. See also Krausnick and Wilhelm, *Truppe*, p. 136.

71 Cited in Walter Manoschek, *'Serbien ist judenfrei'. Militärische Besatzungspolitik und Judenvernichtung in Serbien 1941/42* (R. Oldenbourg Verlag; Munich, 1993), p. 191.

72 See Förster, 'Operation Barbarossa'; Christian Gerlach, *Kalkulierte Morde. Die Deutsche Wirtschafts- und Vernichtungspolitik in Weißrußland 1941 bis 1944* (Hamburger Edition; Hamburg, 1999); Christoph Dieckmann, 'Der Krieg und die Ermordung der Litauischen Juden', in Herbert (ed.), *Nationalsozialistische Vernichtungspolitik*, pp. 292–329.

73 Longerich, *Politik der Vernichtung*, p. 298, citing Herbert Backe.

74 Götz Aly, *'Final Solution'. Nazi Population Policy and the Murder of the European Jews* (Arnold; London, New York, 1995), p. 201. In 1939 continental Europe required imports of twelve to thirteen million tons of grain a year. This was bound to increase in wartime because of loss of efficiency.

75 Christian Streit, *Keine Kameraden. Die Wehrmacht und die Sowjetischen Kriegsgefangenen* (Deutsche Verlags-Anstalt; Stuttgart, 1978), pp. 142ff; Dieckmann, 'Der Krieg und die Ermordung', p. 318.

76 Reproduced in *Documents on the Holocaust*, p. 378.

77 Echoing the earlier work of Alfred Streim, Ralf Ogorreck believes that

the stress on cooperating with the military meant there would not have been secret instructions in the early weeks. Ogorreck, *Einsatzgruppen*, pp. 95–109; Krausnick believes that the actions that followed showed that the verbal orders must have exceeded written instructions. Krausnick and Wilhelm, *Truppe*, p. 161. Christian Gerlach too believes that some kind of exterminatory intention must have been voiced in pre-meetings at Pretzsch or in Berlin. Gerlach, *Kalkulierte Morde*, pp. 629–30. In similar vein Breitman, *Architect*, p. 164. We know, for example, that Heydrich distinguished between short-term and final goals, but it is not clear whether the final goal was to deport the purged remainder further east – this would fit in with the European deportation plans he had been making since the spring – or to kill the remainder. See Introduction in Peter Witte et al. (eds.), *Der Dienstkalender Heinrich Himmlers 1941/1942* (Christians Verlag; Hamburg, 1999), p. 70.

78 Longerich, *Politik der Vernichtung*, pp. 321–52.

79 Christian Gerlach, 'Die Einsatzgruppe B 1941/2', in Peter Klein (ed.), *Die Einsatzgruppen in der Besetzten Sowjetunion 1941/2* (Edition Hentrich; Berlin, 1997), pp. 52–70, here pp. 57–8.

80 Ogorreck, *Die Einsatzgruppen*, pp. 95–109.

81 The October 1941 report from Einsatzgruppe A suggested that from the start 'the goal of the cleansing operation of the Security Police, in accordance with the fundamental orders, was the most comprehensive elimination of the Jews possible'. Cited in Breitman, *Architect*, p. 169. See also the discussion of Stahlecker's response to Lohse's new directives in Christopher R. Browning, *The Path to Genocide. Essays on Launching the Final Solution* (Cambridge University Press; Cambridge, 1992), pp. 109–110. Browning's interpretation, that Stahlecker's ghetto proposals were cover for murder, seems to me more plausible than Longerich's more literal interpretation. See Longerich, *Politik der Vernichtung*, pp. 394–5.

82 Christian Streit, 'Wehrmacht, Einsatzgruppen, Soviet POWs and Anti-Bolshevism in the Emergence of the Final Solution', in Cesarani, *Final Solution*, pp. 103–18, here p. 106.

83 Gerlach, *Kalkulierte Morde*, p. 573.

84 Kershaw, *Hitler 1936–1945*, p. 469.

85 Dieckmann, 'Der Krieg und die Ermordung, pp. 316–19; Gerlach, *Kalkulierte Morde*, p. 636.

86 Browning, *Path to Genocide*, pp. 105–6; Kershaw, *Hitler 1936–1945*, p. 469; Witte et al. (eds.) *Dienstkalender*, p. 185, n 15.

87 Longerich, *Politik der Vernichtung*, pp. 362–9; Ogorreck, *Die Einsatz-gruppen*, pp. 179–81; Gerlach, *Kalkulierte Morde*, pp. 566ff, 648; Gerlach, 'Die Einsatzgruppe B 1941/2', here pp. 57–8.

88 *Dienstkalender*, p. 71.

3. Mass murder to genocide

1 Czeslaw Madajczyk, 'Hitler's Direct Influence on Decisions Affecting Jews During World War II', in *Yad Vashem Studies* 20 (1990), pp. 53–68.

2 Cited in Richard J. Evans, *Lying About Hitler. History, Holocaust and the David Irving Trial* (Basic Books; New York, 2001), p. 78.

3 Richard Breitman, *The Architect of Genocide. Himmler and the Final Solution* (Alfred A. Knopf; New York, 1991), pp. 159ff; Christian Gerlach, *Kalkulierte Morde. Die Deutsche Wirtschafts- und Vernichtungspolitik in Weißrußland 1941 bis 1944* (Hamburger Edition; Hamburg, 1999), pp. 648–9.

4 Reproduced in translation in Yitzhak Arad, Yisrael Gutman and Abraham Margaliot, *Documents on the Holocaust* (University of Nebraska Press; Lincoln and London/Yad Vashem, Jerusalem, Bison Books Edition, 1999), p. 233.

5 Götz Aly, ' "Judenumsiedlung" '. Überlegungen zur Politischen Vorgesch-ichte des Holocaust', in Ulrich Herbert (ed.), *Nationalsozialistische Vernich-tungspolitik 1939–1945, Neue Forschungen und Kontroversen* (Fischer; Frankfurt am Main, 1998), p. 91; Götz Aly, *'Final Solution'. Nazi Population Policy and the Murder of the European Jews* (Arnold; London, New York, 1995), pp. 171–2.

6 Peter Longerich, *Politik der Vernichtung. Eine Gesamtdarstellung der Nationalsozialistischen Judenverfolgung* (Piper Verlag; Munich and Zürich, 1998), p. 288. Was Hitler still thinking of creating a special territory or did he really have murder in mind? The latter interpretation is possible. Hitler's military adjutant, Gerhard Engel, who after the war published a diary of his experiences using undated notes he had made while in Hitler's service, recorded a comment of Hitler's which he retrospectively dated to February 1941. Asked about the Madagascar Plan, which no longer looked feasible, Hitler said that 'He now had some other – not exactly more friendly – things in mind'. Cited in Raul Hilberg, *The Destruction of the European Jews. Revised and Definitive Edition*, vol. 2 (Holmes and Meier; New York and

London, 1985), p. 399. However, most contemporary evidence suggests that thinking in spring 1941 was about deportations to the Soviet Union.

7 Longerich, *Politik der Vernichtung*, p. 422.

8 Hans Safrian, *Die Eichmann-Männer* (Europa Verlag; Vienna, Zürich, 1993), pp. 108ff.

9 Karin Orth, 'Rudolf Höβ und die "Endlösung" der Judenfrage. Drei Argumente gegen deren Datierung auf den Sommer 1941', in *Werkstatt Geschichte* 18 (1997), pp. 45–58.

10 Ibid., p. 52.

11 Longerich, *Politik der Vernichtung*, p. 424.

12 Ian Kershaw, *Hitler 1936–1945*. Vol. 2, *Nemesis* (Allen Lane The Penguin Press; Harmondsworth, 2000), p. 462.

13 Longerich, *Politik der Vernichtung*, p. 427.

14 Philippe Burrin, *Hitler and the Jews. The Genesis of the Holocaust* (Edward Arnold; London, 1994), p. 101; Dieter Pohl, *Von der 'Judenpolitik' zum Judenmord. Der Distrikt Lublin des Generalgouvernements 1939–1944* (Peter Lang; Frankfurt am Main, Berlin, 1993), p. 87.

15 Kershaw, *Hitler 1936–1945*, p. 46.

16 Pohl, *Von der Judenpolitik*, p. 91–2.

17 Peter Witte, 'Two Decisions Concerning the "Final Solution to the Jewish Question": Deportations to Łódź and Mass Murder in Chelmno', *Holocaust and Genocide Studies* vol. 9 (1995), 3, pp. 318–45, here pp. 319, 323–4; Kershaw, *Hitler 1936–1945*, pp. 472–5.

18 Longerich, *Politik der Vernichtung*, p. 438; Witte, 'Two Decisions', pp. 321–5; Kershaw, *Hitler 1936–1945*, p. 479.

19 Christian Gerlach, 'The Wannsee Conference, the Fate of German Jews and Hitler's Decision in Principle to Exterminate All European Jews', in Omer Bartov (ed.), *The Holocaust. Origins, Implementation, Aftermath* (Routledge; London and New York, 2000), pp. 106–61, here p. 110.

20 Christian Gerlach, 'Die Ausweitung der Deutschen Massenmorde in den Besetzten Sowjetischen Gebieten im Herbst 1941. Überlegungen zur Vernichtungspolitik gegen Juden und Sowjetische Kriegsgefangene', in Christian Gerlach, *Krieg, Ernährung, Völkermord. Deutsche Vernichtungspolitik im Zweiten Weltkrieg* (Pendo Verlag; Zürich, Munich, 2001), pp. 11–78, here p. 72.

21 Stalin had announced the decisions at the end of August. Longerich, *Politik der Vernichtung*, pp. 429–30.

22 See Witte, 'Two Decisions', pp. 321–6; Claudia Steur, *Theodor Dannecker. Ein Funktionär der 'Endlösung'* (Klartext Verlag; Essen, 1997), pp. 63–5; Longerich, *Politik der Vernichtung*, p. 430; Kershaw, *Hitler 1936–1945*, p. 478.

23 Above all Burrin, *Hitler and the Jews.*

24 Walter Manoschek, *'Serbien ist judenfrei.' Militärische Besatzungspolitik und Judenvernichtung in Serbien 1941/42* (R. Oldenbourg Verlag; Munich, 1993), pp. 185–7; Pohl, *Von der Judenpolitik*, p. 94; Gerlach, *Kalkulierte Morde*, pp. 646–51; Longerich, *Politik der Vernichtung*, p. 443; Witte, 'Two Decisions', p. 322. It is possible that the orders to build the camp at Sobibor were also given at this time and also just possible that exploratory moves were being made to construct a gas camp in Eastern Galicia near Lvov. Thomas Sandkühler, *'Endlösung' in Galizien. Der Judenmord in Ostpolen und die Rettungsinitiativen von Bertold Beitz 1941–1944* (J. H. W. Dietz Nachfolger; Bonn, 1996). There is some dispute about the Auschwitz date. See Franciszek Piper, 'Gas Chambers and Crematoria', in Yisrael Gutman and Michael Berenbaum, *Anatomy of the Auschwitz Death Camp* (Indiana University Press; Bloomington and Indianapolis, 1994), pp. 157–82, 157, 176, n. 6, but also Jean-Claude Pressac, 'The machinery of mass murder at Auschwitz', in Gutman and Barenbaum, *Anatomy*, pp. 183–245, here p. 242, n 62 and Karin Orth, *Das System der Nationalsozialistischen Konzentrationslager. Eine Politische Organisationsgeschichte* (Hamburger Edition; Hamburg, 1999), p. 139. Orth shows the links between the gassings and the euthanasia/ Soviet POW actions in 'Rudolf Höß', pp. 49–51.

25 Wolfgang Scheffler, 'Chelmno, Sobibor, Belzec und Majdanek', in Eberhard Jäckel and Jürgen Rohwer, *Der Mord an den Juden im Zweiten Weltkrieg* (Deutsche Verlags-Anstalt; Stuttgart, 1985), pp. 145–52, here p. 148.

26 Koeppen's information was indirect on this occasion and it is very possible that it dated back to the time before the deportation decision, and the deportation itself was the 'reprisal'; but possible too that Hitler still held back with an eye on Roosevelt, even though losing faith in the chances of averting US entry into the war. John Lukacs, *The Hitler of History* (Vintage Books; New York, 1997), p. 192; Longerich, *Politik der Vernichtung*, p. 431.

27 Kershaw, *Hitler 1936–1945*, p. 479.

28 On Hitler's perception of the military situation see Christopher R. Browning, *The Path to Genocide. Essays on Launching the Final Solution* (Holmes and Meier, New York, 1985), pp. 112–17.

29 Aly, 'Final Solution', p. 231.

30 Gerlach, Kalkulierte Morde, pp. 618–19.

31 Manoschek, 'Serbien ist judenfrei', pp. 185–90.

32 Ibid., p. 188.

33 Peter Witte et al. (eds.), Der Dienstkalender Heinrich Himmlers 1941/1942 (Christians Verlag; Hamburg, 1999), p. 66; Gerlach, Kalkulierte Morde, p. 186. Dieter Pohl, Nationalsozialistische Judenverfolgung in Ostgalizien 1941–1944. Organisation and Durchführung eines Staatlichen Massenverbrechens (Oldenbourg; Munich, 1996), pp. 140ff; Sandkühler, 'Endlösung' in Galizien, pp. 138–40; Longerich, Politik der Vernichtung, p. 455.

34 Witte et al. (eds.), Dienstkalender, pp. 201–2; Pohl, Nationalsozialistische Judenverfolgung, pp. 140–43; Sandkühler, 'Endlösung' in Galizien, pp. 151–2, 407.

35 On 16 July 1941 the SD in the Wartheland requested the extermination of Jews unable to work. Madajczyk, 'Hitler's Direct Influence', p. 56, note 12. In Latvia there were rumours in early August that the Germans intended to gas Jewish women there. See Breitman, Architect, pp. 160ff and Gerlach, Kalkulierte Morde, pp. 648–9.

36 Höppner memorandum of 16 July is reproduced in Raul Hilberg, Documents of Destruction. Germany and Jewry 1933–1945 (W. H. Allen; London, 1972), p. 87.

37 Cited in Burrin, Hitler and the Jews, p. 119.

38 Ian Kershaw, 'Improvised Genocide? The Emergence of the "Final Solution" in the Warthegau', Transactions of the Royal Historical Society 6th series (1992), pp. 51–78; Deborah Dwork and Robert Jan van Pelt, Auschwitz. 1270 to the Present (W. W. Norton; New York and London, 1996), p. 294.

39 Bogdan Musial, Deutsche Zivilverwaltung und Judenverfolgung im Generalgouvernement (Harrassowitz; Wiesbaden, 1999), p. 195.

40 Sandkühler, 'Endlösung' in Galizien, pp. 138–140.

41 Pohl, Von der Judenpolitik, pp. 99–100; Witte et al. (eds.), Dienstkalender, p. 233 and n 35; Sandkühler, 'Endlösung' in Galizien, p. 136; Bogdan Musial, 'The Origins of "Operation Reinhard": The Decision-making Process for the Mass Murder of the Jews in the Generalgouvernement', Yad Vashem Studies 28 (2000), pp. 113–53, here pp. 116–18.

42 Pohl, Von der Judenpolitik, pp. 105–6; Aly, 'Final Solution', p. 232. Musial, 'Origins', p. 145.

43 See Hitler's comments conveyed to Lammers in the Reich Chancellery

by Martin Bormann, in Helmut Krausnick and Hans-Heinrich Wilhelm, *Die Truppe des Weltanschauungskrieges: die Einsatzgruppen der Sicherheitspolizei und des SD, 1938–1942* (Deutsche Verlags-Anstalt; Stuttgart, 1981), p. 627.

44 Cited in Richard J. Evans, *Lying About Hitler. History, Holocaust and the David Irving Trial* (Basic Books; New York, 2001), p. 88.

45 H. G. Adler, *Der Verwaltete Mensch. Studien zur Deportation der Juden aus Deutschland* (J. C. B. Mohr (Paul Siebeck); Tübingen, 1974), p. 62.

46 Kershaw, *Hitler 1936–1945*, p. 484.

47 Heydrich's statement reproduced in Hans-Günther Adler, *Theresienstadt 1941–1945, Das Antlitz einer Zwangsgemeinschaft. Geschichte. Soziologie. Psychologie.* (J. C. B. Mohr/Paul Siebeck; Tübingen, 1955), p. 720–22.

48 Heydrich said that Nebe and Rasch (commanders of EGB and EGC respectively) could take Jews into the 'camps for communist prisoners in the operation area', Burrin, *Hitler and the Jews*, p. 128.

49 Gerlach, *Kalkulierte Morde*, p. 650.

50 See n. 47; see also Sandkühler, *'Endlösung' in Galizien*, p. 135.

51 The document is cited in Gerald Fleming, *Hitler and the Final Solution* (Oxford University Press; Oxford paperback edition, 1986), pp. 70–71.

52 See Uwe Dietrich Adam, *Judenpolitik im Dritten Reich* (Droste Verlag; Düsseldorf, 1972), p. 309, citing Serge Lang and Ernst von Schenk, *Portrait eines Menscheitsverbrechers. Aus den Hinterlassenen Memorien des Ehemaligen Reichsministers Alfred Rosenberg* (St Gallen; 1947), p. 129; and the discussion in Christopher Browning, *Nazi Policy, Jewish Workers, German Killers* (Cambridge University Press; Cambridge, 2000), pp. 48–9 and Witte et al. (eds.), *Dienstkalender*, p. 262, n 46.

53 Cited in Adler, *Verwaltete Mensch*, p. 63.

54 Kershaw, *Hitler 1936–1945*, p. 485, citing Goebbels's diary.

55 Werner Jochmann (ed.), *Adolf Hitler. Monologe im Führer-Hauptquartier 1941–1944* (Albrecht Kanus Verlag; Hamburg, 1980), pp. 30–31; see the discussion in Evans, *Lying About Hitler*, p. 72.

56 Kershaw, *Hitler 1936–1945*, p. 488. The odd comment about the Jewish state reminds us that Hitler was attempting to make contact with Arab leaders at this time.

57 Kershaw, *Hitler 1936–1945*, p. 478.

58 Shlomo Aronson, 'Hitlers Judenpolitik, die Alliierten und die Juden',

in *Vierteljahrshefte für Zeitgeschichte*, vol. 32 (1984), 1, pp. 29–65, here pp. 51–2.

59 Fleming, *Hitler and the Final Solution*, p. 104.

60 This point seems to me the weakness of Christian Gerlach's otherwise pertinent questions about Hitler's statement to the Grand Mufti. See his discussion in Gerlach, *Krieg, Ernährung*, p. 147, n 240.

61 Longerich, *Politik der Vernichtung*, pp. 434 and 449; Gerlach, *Kalkulierte Morde*, p. 751.

62 For David Irving this telephone message proved Hitler's opposition to murders of the Jews as a whole! David Irving, *Hitler's War* (Viking Press; New York), p. 505.

63 English translation in Richard Breitman, *Official Secrets. What the Nazis Planned. What the British and Americans Knew* (Allen Lane The Penguin Press; London, 1998), p. 82.

64 Breitman, *Official Secrets*, p. 82, drawing on the testimonies collected by Fleming, *Hitler and the Final Solution*.

65 Goebbels's diary entry for 22 November 1941, cited in Evans, *Lying About Hitler*, p. 76.

66 Bernhard Lösener, 'Dokumentation. Das Reichsministerium des Innern und die Judengesetzgebung', in *Vierteljahrshefte für Zeitgeschichte*, vol. 19 (1961), p. 310.

4. The villa, the lake, the meeting

1 On Heydrich, Günther Deschner, *Reinhard Heydrich. Statthalter der Totalen Macht. Biographie* (Bechtle Verlag; Esslingen am Neckar, 1977), Shlomo Aronson, *Reinhard Heydrich und die Frühgeschichte von Gestapo und SD* (Deutsche Verlags-Anstalt; Stuttgart, 1971); Ulrich Herbert, *Best. Biographische Studien über Radikalismus, Weltanschauung und Vernunft, 1903–1989* (J. H. W. Dietz Verlag; Bonn, 1966).

2 Text of the invitation reproduced in Kurt Pätzold and Erika Schwarz, *Tagesordnung: Judenmord. Die Wannsee-Konferenz am 20. Januar 1942* (Metropol; Berlin, 1992), p. 89.

3 Peter Klein, *Die Wannsee-Konferenz vom 20. Januar 1942. Analyse und Dokumentation* (Gedenkstätte Haus der Wannsee-Konferenz, Edition Hentrich; Berlin, no date [1995]), p. 31.

4 Pencilled notation makes clear that the address was changed. The prosecutor at Nuremberg, Robert M. W. Kempner, claimed wrongly to have identified Eichmann's handwriting. Kempner, *Eichmann und Komplizien* (Europa Verlag; Zürich, Stuttgart, Vienna, 1961), p. 129. We do not know whether the first address was given in error or whether Heydrich changed his mind and sought a new venue. Klein, *Die Wannsee-Konferenz*, p. 8.

5 See the list of invitees in the invitations to Luther and Meyer, reproduced in Pätzold and Schwarz, *Tagesordnung: Judenmord*, pp. 88-90.

6 Following the convention in existing translations, Staatssekretär has been rendered here as 'state secretary'. In normal English usage 'secretaries of state' are, of course, ministers, which these men were definitely not. They were, however, political appointments, and in that sense closer to the under-secretary of state.

7 Robert Kempner, *Das Dritte Reich im Kreuzverhör. Aus den Vernehmungs-protokollen des Anklägers* (Athenäum/Droste Taschenbücher; Königstein/Taunus, 1980), p. 189. Kempner was interrogating Erich Neumann at the time.

8 E.g., Martin Gilbert, *Holocaust Journey*, p. 43.

9 Though there are some odd omissions in this case, notably the Führer Chancellery and the army.

10 We can surmise it was before 28 November because a memorandum from Adolf Eichmann notes that, following Friedrich-Wilhelm Krüger's visit on 28 November, it was decided to revise the list slightly. Memorandum reproduced in Pätzold and Schwarz, *Tagesordnung: Judenmord*, p. 90.

11 There is some uncertainty about who exactly was to be invited. We find a memo from Eichmann to the effect that Hans Frank's deputy, Josef Bühler, and HSSPF Krüger were to be added to the list. The list of guests to be found in the invitations sent out on 29 November, however, includes Bühler's boss, Hans Frank (and not Bühler), as well as Krüger. In the list of guests to be found in the note sent to Krüger a couple of days later, on 1 December, Bühler was back in, rather than Frank. The wording of the draft note to Krüger on the 1st suggests also that Krüger himself was in the end not invited. See the invitations reproduced in Pätzold and Schwarz, *Tagesordnung: Judenmord*, pp. 89-90; and above all Klein, *Die Wannsee-Konferenz*, pp, 29-30. See also Gerlach, 'Wannsee', p. 116 and see below, n 36.

12 We do not know exactly when Heydrich ordered his subordinates to attend. It is possible that Lange from the Soviet Union was a late addition.

13 Lösener, 'Reichsministerium', p. 297.

14 Christian Gerlach, 'The Wannsee Conference, the Fate of German Jews and Hitler's Decision in Principle to Exterminate All European Jews', in Omer Bartov (ed.), *The Holocaust. Origins, Implementation, Aftermath* (Routledge; London and New York, 2000), p. 119; Beate Meyer, *'Jüdische Mischlinge', Rassenpolitik und Verfolgungserfahrung 1933–1945* (Dölling und Galitz Verlag; Hamburg, 1999), pp. 90ff.

15 See the memo 'Wünsche und Ideen des Auswärtigen Amtes zu der Vorgesehenen Gesamtlösung der Judenfrage in Europa' drawn up by Referat DIII for Martin Luther, 8 December 1941, reproduced in Pätzold and Schwarz, *Tagesordnung: Judenmord*, p. 91.

16 Henry R. Huttenbach, 'The Wannsee Conference Reconsidered 50 Years After: SS Strategy and Racial Politics in the Third Reich', in Hubert Locke and Marcia Littell, *Remembrance and Recollection. Essays on the Centennial Year of Martin Niemöller and Reinhold Niebühr and the 50th Year of the Wannsee Conference* (University Press of America; Lanham, New York, London, 1996), pp. 58–79, here p. 60 suggests that we know Heydrich agreed at this stage to put Foreign Office matters on the agenda. I think this is based on a misunderstanding of a rather ambiguous reference to 'his subordinates' (meaning Luther's not Heydrich's) in Richard Breitman, *The Architect of Genocide. Himmler and the Final Solution* (Alfred A. Knopf; New York, 1991), pp. 224–5. Raul Hilberg suggests that Heinrich Lammers, the well-informed minister in charge of the Reich Chancellery, believed that the proceedings were of broader significance still, saying that Lammers told his subordinates to watch out for forthcoming invitations from the RSHA to make sure they attended as a 'listening post'. However, this comment I think is based on Lammers's rather muddled testimony from 1946. His later testimony makes clear that this particular instruction followed rather than preceded Wannsee and was meant to imply that the Reich Chancellery should play a very limited role. See Lammers's testimony from 8.4.1946, reproduced in Pätzold and Schwarz, *Tagesordnung: Judenmord*, p. 133; later testimony in *Trials of War Criminals Before the Nuremberg Military Tribunals Under Control Council Law No. 10*, Volumes 13–15: *'The Ministries Case'*, (Nuremberg, October 1946–April 1949), vol. 13, p. 414 and see also Dieter Rebentisch, *Führerstaat und Verwaltung im Zweiten Weltkrieg. Verfassungsentwicklung und Verwaltungspolitik 1939–1945* (Franz Steiner Verlag; Stuttgart, 1989), pp. 434ff.

17 We deduce they telephoned because we know that until the 8th the participants still believed the meeting would go ahead. On that day Luther's subordinate Rademacher presented him with notes 'for tomorrow's meeting'. Hans Safrian, *Die Eichmann-Männer* (Europa Verlag; Vienna, Zürich, 1993), p. 169. Since the cancellation does not appear in the otherwise complete Foreign Office records of the meeting, it was probably made by phone.

18 Officials in the Interior Ministry believed that it was the forthcoming Reichstag session that originally led to Wannsee's postponement. See the Ministry of the Eastern Territories memo reproduced in Klein, *Die Wannsee-Konferenz*, p. 40.

19 My translation of Goebbels, entry for 13 December 1941, cited in Christian Gerlach, *Krieg, Ernährung. Völkermord. Deutsche Vernichtungspolitik im Zweiten Weltkrieg* (Pendo Verlag; Zürich, Munich, 2001), p, 114,

20 Frank's speech, cited in Gerlach, *Krieg, Ernährung*, p. 122.

21 This is a reference to the forthcoming Wannsee meeting. The text of Frank's speech was known at the time of the War Crimes Trial, 1945-6, and was in fact to be the first hint for the Allies of the existence of the Wannsee meeting.

22 My translation from Gerlach, *Krieg, Ernährung*, p. 112.

23 My translation from Werner Jochmann (ed.) *Adolf Hitler. Monologe im Führer-Hauptquartier 1941-1944* (Albrecht Kanus Verlag; Hamburg, 1980), p. 229.

24 Ibid., p. 263.

25 A point well made by Ian Kershaw, *Hitler 1936-1945*. Vol. 2, *Nemesis* (Allen Lane The Penguin Press; Harmondsworth, 2000), p. 487.

26 Gerlach argues that the 'decision' to which Rosenberg refers must be about the Jews, rather than the decision to go to war with the USA, since there was no logical reason for the onset of hostilities with the US to prevent the minister from discussing anti-Jewish measures.

27 See the discussion in Gerlach, 'Wannsee', p. 150, fn 109 and Christopher R. Browning, *Nazi Policy, Jewish Workers, German Killers* (Cambridge University Press; Cambridge, 2000), p. 54, n 78.

28 Reproduced in Klein, *Die Wannsee-Konferenz*, p. 38.

29 Kershaw, *Hitler 1936-1945*, pp. 450-57.

30 'Die Villenkolonien in Berlin-Wannsee 1870-1945', in Gedenkstätte Haus der Wannsee-Konferenz (ed.) *Villenkolonien in Wannsee 1870-1945. Groß-*

bürgerliche Lebenswelt und Ort der Wannsee-Konferenz (Edition Hentrich; Berlin, 2000), pp. 14–69; Norbert Kampe, 'Zur Ausstellung im Garten der Gedenkstätte', in *Villenkolonien*, pp. 8–13; Gideon Botsch, 'Der SD in Berlin-Wannsee 1937–1945. Wannsee-Institut, Institut für Staatsforschung und Gästehaus der Sicherheitspolizei und des SD', in *Villenkolonien*, pp. 70–95.

31 Contrary to speculation, Minoux had not financed Hitler.

32 Johannes Tuchel, *Am Großen Wannsee 56–58. Von der Villa Minoux zum Haus der Wannsee-Konferenz* (Edition Hentrich; Berlin, 1992), pp. 38, 76, 96.

33 Ibid., pp. 105–8.

34 Including Heydrich but excluding the stenotypist and Günther, if he was present.

35 Raul Hilberg, *Destruction of the European Jews*, vol. 2, (Holmes and Meier; New York and London, 1985) p. 421.

36 See also note 11. In terms of rank, Krüger and not Schöngarth was the appropriate counterpart to Bühler. Yet the wording of the (draft) note to Krüger suggests that he was never invited. Peter Klein speculates that Schöngarth was invited as a more politic guest, given the well-known and long-standing animosity between Krüger and Frank/Bühler. Klein, *Die Wannsee-Konferenz*, pp. 13–14; see also Raul Hilberg, *Perpetrators, Victims, Bystanders. The Jewish Catastrophe 1933–1945* (HarperCollins; London, 1992), p. 48. Another virtue of Schöngarth, from Heydrich's point of view, was that in the complicated SS/Security Police structure Schöngarth, though Krüger's subordinate, was also answerable to Heydrich, unlike Krüger who, as HSSPF, was directly answerable to Himmler.

37 Adolf Eichmann, 'Götzen', unpublished manuscript (Haifa, 1961), p. 219.

38 'Das Protokoll dieser Konferenz war lang, obgleich ich das Unwesentliche nicht einmal hatte stenographieren lassen', in Eichmann, 'Götzen', p. 226.

39 *Trials of War Criminals*, vol. 13, p. 414.

40 See the note from Rosenberg's racial expert, Erhard Wetzel, on the *Mischling* discussion, which suggested it had been exploratory only, in Götz Aly and Susanne Heim, *Vordenker der Vernichtung: Auschwitz und die Deutschen Pläne für eine Neue Europäische Ordnung* (Hoffmann und Campe; Hamburg, 1991), p. 470. This is explored in greater detail on p. 100.

41 The original can be found in the Politisches Archiv des Auswärtigen Amtes, Berlin, Ref Inland IIg/177/165–80. The best facsimile of the original

Protocol is in Peter Klein, 'Die Wannsee-Konferenz', in *Villenkolonien in Wannsee 1870–1945*, pp. 96–136.

42 The German in the original here is slightly odd. In the phrase '*erfordert die vorherige gemeinsame Behandlung aller an diesen Fragen beteiligten Zentralinstanzen*' (dealing together with all the central bodies involved in these questions), one would expect the object of the term 'dealing with' (*Behandlung*) to be the questions raised by the Jewish problem. Instead, the grammar of the sentence makes clear that it is the organizations (*Instanzen*) involved in such questions who need to be dealt with together. It seems the Protocol itself misquotes Heydrich's own earlier note from 29 November 1941 and unwittingly reveals his desire to take control of the other authorities.

43 See Eichmann's comments at his trial, Session 79, 12 June 1961.

44 '. . . *gewisse vorbereitende Arbeiten im Zuge der Endlösung gleich in den betreffenden Gebieten selbst durchzuführen*'.

45 Kershaw, *Hitler 1936–1945*, p. 493.

46 Pätzold and Schwarz, *Tagesordnung: Judenmord*, p. 57.

47 Reproduced in Kempner, *Eichmann und Komplizien*, pp. 152–3.

48 Robert M. W. Kempner, *Ankläger einer Epoche. Lebenserinnerungen* (Ullstein; Frankfurt am Main, Berlin, Vienna, 1983), p. 339.

49 Hans Mommsen, 'The Realization of the Unthinkable: The "Final Solution of the Jewish Question" in the Third Reich', in Hans Mommsen, *From Weimar to Auschwitz. Essays in German History* (Basil Blackwell; Oxford, 1991), p. 249; Hans Mommsen, 'Aufgabenkreis und Verantwortlichkeit des Staatssekretärs der Reichskanzlei Dr Wilhelm Kritzinger', in Institut für Zeitgeschichte (ed.), *Gutachten*, vol. 2 (Deutsche Verlags-Anstalt; Stuttgart, 1966), pp. 369–98, here p. 381; Dieter Rebentisch, *Führerstaat und Verwaltung im Zweiten Weltkrieg. Verfassungsentwicklung und Verwaltungspolitik 1939–1945* (Franz Steiner Verlag; Stuttgart, 1989), p. 439.

50 My translation from Bernhard Lösener, 'Dokumentation. Das Reichsministerium des Innern und die Judengesetzgebung', in *Vierteljahrshefte für Zeitgeschichte*, vol. 19 (1961), p. 297.

51 *Trials of War Criminals*, vol. 14, p. 642.

52 Uwe Dietrich Adam, *Judenpolitik im Dritten Reich* (Droste Verlag; Düsseldorf, 1972), p. 315.

53 'I would reckon today that it was prepared about two weeks, three weeks, I would reckon today, before the beginning of the date originally scheduled in December 1941', Eichmann Trial, session 106, 21 July 1961.

54 See Klein, *Die Wannsee-Konferenz*, p. 5. Wolfgang Scheffler, 'Die Wann-see-Konferenz und Ihre Historische Bedeutung', in the brochure edited by Gedenkstätte Haus der Wannsee-Konferenz, 'Erinnern für die Zukunft' (printed by the Gedenkstätte, Berlin, no date [1992], p. 24. I am very grateful to Peter Klein for providing additional guidance here, though it seems there is still some ambiguity as to the exact scope of Eichmann's instruction.

55 Originally, Eichmann did, it is true, say that he learned about the plan to murder the Jews around the turn of the year 1941–2. He later not very convincingly backdated this to summer 1941. What he did not do, however, was place the Wannsee meeting in the context of a major change of Hitler's policy.

56 Peter Longerich, 'The Wannsee Conference in the Development of the "Final Solution"' (Holocaust Educational Trust Research Papers, vol. 1, no. 2, London, 2000), pp. 13–14.

57 The oddity in this context is Bühler and Meyer calling for measures to be taken 'directly in the countries concerned'. But the statement is so ambiguous that it cannot really influence our conclusions. It may mean that they thought deportations *to* their respective territories should not include too many Jews who could be 'dealt with' before being shipped off.

58 Cited in Raul Hilberg, *Documents of Destruction. Germany and Jewry 1933–1945* (W. H. Allen; London, 1972), p. 104.

59 See Raul Hilberg, *Perpetrators, Victims, Bystanders. The Jewish Catastrophe 1933–1945* (HarperCollins; London, 1992), p. 49.

60 This too is Mommsen's view, 'Aufgabenkreis', p. 380. Rebentisch's view that the conference did not make clear what was at stake and that the Protocol was purely for internal RSHA purposes I find absolutely incomprehensible, in view of the Protocol's contents, the fact that it was attached to the invitation to subsequent meetings, and Lammers's own early admission of having received it. See Rebentisch, *Führerstaat*, p. 439.

61 Interrogation of Lammers 8 April 1946 as a witness in the Nuremberg Trials; interrogation of Lammers as accused in the Ministries Trial, September 1948, interrogation of Wilhelm Stuckart by his defence counsel in the Ministries Trial, 6 October 1948 all reproduced in Pätzold and Schwarz, *Tagesord-nung: Judenmord*, pp. 132, 154, 156–8. On the first occasion, Lammers misremembered the date, referring to a meeting in 1943, but it is clearly the Wannsee conference.

62 In this respect John Grenville's interpretation of Wannsee – that the

non-Jewish slave reservoir seemed to Heydrich inexhaustible and Jewish labour expendable – is, I believe not tenable. See John A. S. Grenville, 'Die "Endlösung" und die "Judenmischlinge" im Dritten Reich', in Ursula Büttner with Werner Johe and Angelika Voss (eds.), *Das Unrechtsregime: Internationale Forschung über den Nationalsozialismus* (Christians Verlag; Hamburg, 1986).

63 Certainly, there were local variations. In Łódź, (in the Wartheland rather than the Generalgouvernement), the authorities used the ghetto as a productive enterprise whereas in the Warsaw ghetto it was only for a brief period in 1941 that a similar approach was adopted. By then, hunger and disease were killing off the ghetto population. See Christopher Browning, 'Nazi Ghettoization Policy in Poland', in Christopher R. Browning, *The Path to Genocide. Essays on Launching the Final Solution* (Holmes and Meier; New York, 1985), pp. 28–58.

64 Christian Gerlach, *Kalkulierte Morde. Die Deutsche Wirtschafts- und Vernichtungspolitik in Weißrußland 1941 bis 1944* (Hamburger Edition; Hamburg, 1999), p. 582.

65 Pohl, *Nationalsozialistische Judenverfolgung*, pp. 165ff; Sandkühler, *'Endlösung' in Galizien*, p. 134.

66 In fact, of course, the Nazis' murderous approach – as the example of the Generalgouvernement shows – made it impossible to utilize labour rationally. The circle could not be squared in this way. The fact remains, as Yisrael Gutman reminds us, that the few Jews who survived in the camps owed their lives largely to the Germans' need for manpower. Yisrael Gutman, 'Auschwitz – an overview', in Gutman and Berenbaum, *Anatomy*, pp. 5–33, here p. 9.

67 Mommsen, 'Realization', p. 248.

68 John Grenville is one of a number of historians who have shown that these borderline cases formed the real *policy* content of Wannsee. Grenville, '"Endlösung"', p. 108. See also Jeremy Noakes, 'The Development of Nazi Policy Towards the German-Jewish "Mischlinge"', in *Leo Baeck Institute Year Book* 34 (1989), pp. 291–356, here p. 341.

69 Stuckart's testimony reproduced in Pätzold and Schwarz, *Tagesordnung: Judenmord*, p. 158.

70 Jeremy Noakes, 'Wohin Gehören die "Judenmischlinge"? Die Entstehung der Ersten Durchführungsverordnungen zu den Nürnberger Gesetzen', in Büttner, Johe and Voss (eds.), *Das Unrechtsregime*, pp. 69–89; Hilberg, *Destruction of the European Jews*, vol. 1, pp. 68–74.

71 See Lösener, 'Reichsministerium', pp. 272, 306. Evidence of the importance of his role is that Interior Ministry policy where he was not involved was often far closer to that of the Party radicals. See the question of half-Jewish youngsters in local authority care, in Adam, *Judenpolitik* , pp. 223–4. Hilberg, *Destruction of the European Jews*, vol. 1, p. 71.

72 See Grenville, ' "Endlösung" '; Hilberg, *Destruction of the European Jews*, vol. 2, p. 419, fn 7.

73 Noakes, ' "Judenmischlinge" ', p. 69.

74 Hilberg, *Destruction of the European Jews*, vol. 1, p. 70, fn 11.

75 The terms first and second degree entered the legal definition only later.

76 Hilberg, *Destruction of the European Jews*, vol. 1, p. 72.

77 Noakes, ' "Judenmischlinge" ', pp. 85–6.

78 Noakes, 'Development', p. 337; Adam, *Judenpolitik*, p. 218; Meyer, '*Jüdische Mischlinge*', pp. 30–31.

79 See report by Fred K. Salter from US Consulate General, reproduced in Mendelsohn, *Holocaust*, vol. 13, *The Judicial System and the Jews in Nazi Germany*, pp. 1–32.

80 Noakes, 'The Development of Nazi Policy', pp. 291–356, here p. 339; Lösener, 'Reichsministerium', p. 297.

81 Above all the Führer Chancellery and the military.

82 Grenville, ' "Endlösung" ', pp. 109–10.

83 Meyer, '*Jüdische Mischlinge*', p. 25.

84 Hilberg, *Destruction of the European Jews*, vol. 2, p. 418.

85 Scheffler, 'Wannsee-Konferenz', pp. 18, 23, 26; Walter Hagen, *Die Geheime Front* (Linz, Vienna; 1950), p. 24, cited in Gerald Reitlinger, *Final Solution: The Attempt to Exterminate the Jews of Europe, 1939–1945*, pp. 102, 550, n 10; Eberhard Jäckel, 'On the Purpose of the Wannsee Conference', in James S. Pacy and Alan P. Wertheimer (eds.), *Perspectives on the Holocaust. Essays in Honor of Raul Hilberg* (Westview Press; Boulder, San Francisco, Oxford, 1995), p. 45.

86 Scheffler, 'Wannsee-Konferenz', p. 18; Reitlinger, *Final Solution*, p. 102.

87 Eichmann's testimony from 1 June 1960, reproduced in Pätzold and Schwarz, *Tagesordnung: Judenmord*, pp. 162–3.

88 Jäckel, 'Purpose', p. 45.

89 My translation from Tuchel, *Am Großen Wannsee*, p. 121.

90 See p. 50.

91 Peter Witte et al. (eds.), *Der Dienstkalender Heinrich Himmlers 1941/1942* (Christians Verlag; Hamburg, 1999), p. 265.

92 Ibid., p. 274.

93 Ibid., p. 277.

94 Eichmann Trial, session 78.

95 Hans Safrian, *Die Eichmann-Männer* (Europa Verlag; Vienna, Zürich, 1993), pp. 143–7, especially p. 146.

96 Hilberg, *Perpetrators*, p. 48–9.

97 George C. Browder, *Foundations of the Nazi Police State. The Formation of SIPO and SD* (The University Press of Kentucky; Lexington, 1990), p. 229; Lösener, 'Reichsministerium', p. 286.

98 Hilberg, 'Documents of destruction', p. 104.

99 Cited in Gerlach, 'Wannsee', p. 120.

100 Eichmann Trial, session 10, 19 April 1961.

101 Information from Pätzold, *Judenmord*, pp. 201ff.

102 Pätzold, *Judenmord*, pp. 201ff; Helmut Ortner, *Der Hinrichter. Roland Freisler – Mörder im Dienste Hitlers* (Zsolnay Verlag; Vienna, 1993), p. 51, 60.

103 Robert Wistrich, *Who's Who in Nazi Germany* (Weidenfeld and Nicolson; London, 1982), p. 310; Herbert, *Best*, pp. 284–5; *Trials of War Criminals*, vol. 14, pp. 631–2; Rebentisch, *Führerstaat*, pp. 109, 545.

104 Rebentisch, *Führerstaat*, p. 318.

105 Ibid.

106 Freisler, Meyer and Stuckart.

107 Bühler, Schöngarth, Leibbrandt. This information, and that in the preceding note, from Pätzold and Schwarz, *Tagesordnung: Judenmord*, pp. 201ff.

108 Herbert, *Best*, p. 285.

109 Ibid., p. 284.

110 H. W. Koch, *In the Name of the Volk. Political Justice in Hitler's Germany* (I. B. Tauris; London, 1989), p. 31.

111 Ortner, *Der Hinrichter*, p. 101.

112 Browder, *Foundations of the Nazi Police State*, p. 185.

113 Politische Beurteilung des Kriminal-Oberinspektors Heinrich Müller durch die Gauleitung München-Oberbayeren, Amt für Beamte, 4.1.1937, signed Otto Nippold, deputy Gauleiter Münich-Oberbayern, cited in Aronson, *Heydrich*, p. 321.

114 Browning, *Foreign Office*, p. 27.

115 Ibid., p. 28; Reitlinger, *Final Solution*, p. 24.

116 E.g., on Madagascar, Browning, *Foreign Office*; Claudia Steur, *Theodor Dannecker. Ein Funktionär der 'Endlösung'* (Klartext Verlag; Essen, 1997). For Luther and Serbia, see p. 96.

117 Herbert, *Best*, pp. 285–6.

118 The Nuremberg judges (*Trials of War Criminals*, vol. 14, p. 645) were, however, wrong in assuming that Stuckart wrote in 1938 that after the Nuremberg Laws and subsequent codifications, racial legislation was 'essentially complete'. Stuckart did indeed write that 'many of the decisions' already taken would 'lose their importance as the final solution of the Jewish problem' was reached. But this does not appear in the 1938 edition of his legal handbook, 'The Care for Race and Heredity in the Legislation of the Reich', and is added only in the later 1943 edition. I am grateful to Hans-Christian Jasch for pointing this out.

119 See Helmut Großcurth's comments in *Tagebücher eines Abwehroffiziers 1938–1940* (Deutsche Verlagsanstalt; Stuttgart, 1970), p. 162. See also the comments of Heinz Höhne, cited in Deschner, *Heydrich*, p. 174.

120 Aronson, *Heydrich*, pp. 244–54.

121 Rebentisch, *Führerstaat*, p. 544.

122 Mommsen, 'Aufgabenkreis', p. 370.

123 Ibid., p. 389.

124 *Trials of War Criminals*, vol. 14, p. 643.

125 Mommsen, 'Aufgabenkreis', p. 386.

126 Rebentisch, *Führerstaat*, p. 436.

127 See Lösener, 'Reichsministerium'.

128 See Fleming, *Hitler and the Final Solution*, pp. 70–71.

129 Safrian, *Eichmann-Männer*, p. 149.

130 Ronald Headland, *Messages of Murder. A Study of the Reports of the Einsatzgruppen of the Security Police and the Security Service* (Fairleigh Dickinson University Press; Rutherford, Madison, Teaneck, 1992), pp. 46–7, 230.

131 Browning, *Foreign Office*, p. 73.

132 Ibid., p. 74.

133 *Trials of War Criminals*, vol. 14, p. 423.

134 Ibid., p. 640.

135 Lösener, 'Reichsministerium', p. 311.

136 Gerlach, *Kalkulierte Morde*, pp. 544–5.

137 Safrian, *Eichmann-Männer*, p. 142.

138 Pohl, *Von der Judenpolitik*, p. 94.

139 Browning, *Foreign Office*, p. 64.

140 Ibid., pp. 56ff.

5. A largely successful day

1 Raul Hilberg, *The Destruction of the European Jews* (revised and definitive edition), vol. 2 (Holmes and Meier; New York and London, 1985), p. 491.

2 Beate Meyer, *'Jüdische Mischlinge', Rassenpolitik und Verfolgungserfahrung 1933–1945* (Dölling und Galitz Verlag; Hamburg, 1999), p. 98.

3 Testimony reproduced in Kurt Pätzold and Erika Schwarz, *Tagesordnung: Judenmord. Die Wannsee-Konferenz am 20. Januar 1942* (Metropol; Berlin, 1992), p. 156.

4 Hilberg, *Destruction of the European Jews*, vol. 2, p. 420, fn 9; Uwe Dietrich Adam, *Judenpolitik im Dritten Reich* (Droste Verlag; Düsseldorf, 1972), p. 323, fn 100; Meyer, *'Jüdische Mischlinge'*, pp. 98, 404, fn 16.

5 Bernhard Lösener, 'Dokumentation. Das "Reichsministerium" des Innern und die Judengesetzgebung', in *Vierteljahrshefte für Zeitgeschichte*, vol. 19 (1961), p. 298.

6 See the discussion in Meyer, *'Jüdische Mischlinge'*, p. 98.

7 Götz Aly and Susanne Heim, *Vordenker der Vernichtung: Auschwitz und die Deutschen Pläne für eine Neue Europäische Ordnung* (Hoffmann and Campe; Hamburg, 1991), p. 418.

8 Minutes of consultation with Reichsminister Lammers on 2 October 1941, reproduced in John Mendelsohn (ed.), *The Holocaust. Selected Documents in 18 Volumes*, vol. 2: *Legalizing the Holocaust. The Later Phase, 1939–1943* (Garland; New York and London, 1982), pp. 284–6; see also Hilberg, *Destruction of the European Jews*, vol. 2, pp. 418, 420, n 9.

9 Eichmann Trial, session 79, 26 June 1961.

10 Ibid., session 107, 24 July 1961.

11 So-called Sassen interviews. Cited in the Eichmann Trial, session 75, 20 June 1961.

12 Eichmann Trial, session 79, 26 June 1961.

13 Ibid., session 106, 21 July 1961.

14 See also Aly and Heim, *Vordenker*, p. 469.

15 Ibid., p. 470.

16 Robert Kempner, *Eichmann und Komplizien* (Europa Verlag; Zürich, Stuttgart, Vienna, 1961), p. 165; Jeremy Noakes, 'The Development of Nazi Policy Towards the German-Jewish "Mischlinge"', in *Leo Baeck Institute Year Book* 34 (1989), p. 343.

17 Himmler's letter to Gottlob Berger, cited in Noakes, 'Nazi Policy', p. 346.

18 The full minutes of the March and October meetings are reproduced in Kempner, *Eichmann und Komplizien*, pp. 165–80 and pp. 255–67. See also the note on the March meeting from Fritz Rademacher, reproduced in abbreviated form in Pätzold and Schwarz, *Tagesordnung: Judenmord*, p. 119. Full text in the Wiener Library, Microfilm, K195.

19 The Justice Ministry objections are not identified in the minutes but are referred to by Rademacher in his subsequent note of 7 March. Wiener Library, document K195. See Hilberg, *Destruction of the European Jews*, vol. 2, pp. 421–9 and also Noakes's more generous interpretation in 'Nazi Policy', p. 347.

20 At Nuremberg, Lammers's position was not believed, see prosecution summing up from trial of H. Lammers in the Ministries Trial, reproduced in Mendelsohn, *Holocaust*, vol. 18: *The Ohlendorf and Weizsaecker Cases*, p. 106. But the discovery of a memo from Schlegelberger has rather vindicated Lammers's claims on this issue. See Schlegelberger memo in Bundesarchiv file R22/52, cited on David Irving's website. Irving interprets the memo as meaning Hitler rejected the Final Solution as a whole. This is inconsistent not only with Hitler's own remarks but also with his demonstrated ability to stop developments he did not like.

21 Meyer, '*Jüdische Mischlinge*', p. 12.

22 Noakes, 'Nazi Policy', pp. 347–8; Meyer, '*Jüdische Mischlinge*', p. 51.

23 H. G. Adler, *Der Verwaltete Mensch. Studien zur Deportation der Juden aus Deutschland* (J. C. B. Mohr (Paul Siebeck); Tübingen, 1974), pp. 202ff, 280–81.

24 Wolfgang Benz, 'Die Dimension des Völkermords', in Wolfgang Benz (ed.), *Dimension des Völkermords. Die Zahl der Jüdischen Opfer des Nationalsozialismus* (Oldenbourg Verlag; Munich, 1991), pp. 1–23, here p. 17.

25 Christopher R. Browning, *The Path to Genocide. Essays on Launching the Final Solution* (Cambridge University Press; Cambridge, 1992), p. ix.

26 Letter from Heydrich, 25 January 1942 to Befehlshaber der Sicherheitspolizei und des SD among others re 'Final Solution of the Jewish Question', reproduced on the website of the Gedenkstätte Haus der Wannsee-Konferenz, www.ghwk.de/deut/chefsd.htm.

27 My translation from Johannes Tuchel, *Am Großen Wannsee 56–58. Von der Villa Minoux zum Haus der Wannsee-Konferenz* (Edition Hentrich; Berlin, 1992), p. 121; see also Christian Gerlach, 'The Wannsee Conference, the Fate of German Jews and Hitler's Decision in Principle to Exterminate All European Jews', in Omer Bartov (ed.), *The Holocaust. Origins, Implementation, Aftermath* (Routledge; London and New York, 2000), p. 130.

28 Wisliceny's post-war testimony should be taken with more than a pinch of salt. However, these comments were made in Hungary before the end of the war. See Kempner, *Eichmann*, p. 182.

29 Eichmann Trial, session 10, 19 April 1961; see also Gerlach, 'Wannsee', p. 111.

30 Ibid., session 79, 26 June 1961.

31 Hans Safrian, *Die Eichmann-Männer* (Europa Verlag; Vienna, Zürich, 1993), p. 174.

32 Cited in Kempner, *Eichmann*, p. 180.

33 Ibid., p. 148.

34 Kempner, *Eichmann*, p. 148; Christian Gerlach, *Kalkulierte Morde. Die Deutsche Wirtschafts- und Vernichtungspolitik in Weißrußland 1941 bis 1944* (Hamburger Edition; Hamburg, 1999), p. 755.

35 My translation from citation in Aly and Heim, *Vordenker*, p. 460.

36 The invitation, sent out on 26 February, is reproduced in facsimile in Kempner, *Eichmann*, p. 150.

37 The cover note with the Wannsee Protocol is dated 26 February 1942, but it is not certain when the recipients received their copies. Kempner, *Eichmann*, p. 149.

38 Dieter Pohl, *Von der 'Judenpolitik' zum Judenmord. Der Distrikt Lublin des Generalgouvernements 1939–1944* (Peter Lang; Frankfurt am Main, Berlin (1993), p. 109.

39 Ibid., pp. 102, 110.

40 Gerlach, 'Wannsee', p. 139; Gerlach, *Kalkulierte Morde*, p. 755.

41 Dieter Pohl, *Nationalsozialistische Judenverfolgung in Ostgalizien 1941–1944. Organisation und Durchführung eines Staatlichen Masserverbrechens* (Oldenbourg; Munich, 1996), p. 204.

42 Longerich, *Politik der Vernichtung*, p. 488; Yitzhak Arad, *Bełżec, Sobibor, Treblinka. The Operation Reinhard Death Camps* (Indiana University Press; Bloomington and Indianapolis, 1987), pp. 75, 81, 392; Christopher Browning, 'A Final Hitler Decision for the "Final Solution"? The Riegner Telegram Reconsidered', *Holocaust and Genocide Studies*, vol. 10 (1996), 1, pp. 3–10.

43 Peter Witte, 'Two Decisions Concerning the "Final Solution to the Jewish Question": Deportations to Łódź and Mass Murder in Chelmno', *Holocaust and Genocide Studies*, vol. 9 (1995), pp. 333–4; see also Peter Witte et al. (eds.), *Der Dienstkalender Heinrich Himmlers 1941/1942* (Christians Verlag; Hamburg, 1999), pp. 67, 73; Pohl, *Nationalsozialistische Judenverfolgung*, pp. 204–5; Browning, 'A Final Hitler Decision'; Karin Orth, 'Rudolf Höß und die "Endlösung" der Judenfrage. Drei Argumente gegen deren Datierung auf den Sommer 1941', in *Werkstatt Geschichte* 18 (1997), p. 48; Pohl, *Von der Judenpolitik*, p. 128; Gerlach, *Kalkulierte Morde*, pp. 662ff.

44 Eichmann had by this time in the trial shifted from his earlier position that the Final Solution was ordered at the end of the year to the view that the order had originated in the summer of 1941.

45 Eichmann Trial, session 93, 12 July 1961.

46 Herbert, *Best*, p. 320.

Appendix A: The Protocol

1 This translation is a revised version of the translation in John Mendelsohn (ed.), *The Holocaust: Selected Documents in Eighteen Volumes*, vol. 11: *The Wannsee Protocol and a 1944 Report on Auschwitz by the Office of Strategic Services* (Garland; New York, 1982), pp. 3–17, with stylistic improvements and clarifications from Dan Rogers and Mark Roseman.

Index

INDEX